"Dr. Burrus's book is helpful for a boss. Managing Brilliant Jerks *is* *one can easily relate to. It is a must-read if you* *the job with a "jerk." A great tool for these challenging times!"*

—Chérie Carter-Scott, PhD, MCC, Author of *The Corporate Negaholic* and #1 *New York Times* bestselling author of *If Life Is a Game, These Are the Rules*

"This book presents a solid, practical 'how-to' coaching process that can enrich your coaching practice and management abilities to deal with these difficult and sometimes toxic leaders. Dr. Burrus provides a comprehensive coaching guide while weaving a real-life case study throughout the book. It provides both the theory and the practical approach to transform these individuals into productive and effective leaders."

—Damian Goldvarg, PhD, MCC, CSP; President, The Goldvarg Consulting Group, Inc.; Certified Mentor Coach, Accredited Coaching Supervisor; and International Coach Federation Global Past President

"Dr. Burrus has given leaders a license to chill out and a template for doing so in this thoughtfully crafted guide. Managing Brilliant Jerks *calls on us to foster and forge new relationships with leaders who unconsciously intimidate or 'zombify' their workforce. We need this perspective at this time in our history. We need someone to help us label and reframe possibility in a business and political climate where aggression and bullying methods allow for abuse in many positions of leadership. The notion that we can find and unleash a visionary soul lurking behind the façade of even the most challenging leader is more than a compelling idea, as there are real tools and examples for effective use of the methods within. The tone and pace make this a book you will want to read and highlight key sections of each chapter. Keep it handy for your most important assignments and partnerships!"*

—Darelyn "DJ" Mitsch, MCC, Master Team Coach, Catalyst of Awesomeness; Pyramid Resource Group President; and Author of *Zombies to Zealots: Reawaken the Human Spirit at Work*

MANAGING BRILLIANT
Jerks

MANAGING BRILLIANT *Jerks*

How Organizations and Coaches Can Transform Difficult Leaders into *Powerful Visionaries*

KATRINA BURRUS, PhD, MCC

First published by MKB Excellent Executive Coaching
Copyright © 2017 by Katrina Burrus, Ph.D., MCC
First Edition

4950 Mountain Creek Drive
Las Vegas, NV 89148
USA
Tel: +41 79 200 90 92 and +1 702 767 9436

www.ExcellentExecutiveCoaching.com

Cover Design: StyleMatters, LLC, info@style-matters.com
Interior Design: Jerry Dorris, StyleMatters, www.style-matters.com

Library of Congress Control Number: 2017917400

ISBN 978-0-692-51086-5

*This book is dedicated to my mother,
Mary Barbey, who believed in me, and to my
children: Christelle and John-Kelly Burrus.
May they find their passion in life. Special
thanks also to Christophe Burrus.*

Table of Contents

Acknowledgements — *xi*

Introduction — *xiii*

Chapter 1 — Case Study: *When Bright Leaders Become Abrasive Jerks* — 1

Chapter 2 — Brilliant Jerks' DNA: *Who Are They? How Can They Be Identified?* — 11

Chapter 3 — What Does It Take to Be a Successful Leader? *The Key Differences Between Abrasive and Demanding Leaders* — 21

Chapter 4 — Toxic Behavior Is a Virus: *What Are the Abrasive Jerk's Insidious Effects on Individuals, Teams, and Organizations?* — 33

Chapter 5 — Treating the Virus: *How Organizations Can Encourage Healthy Behavior at the Organization, Team, and Individual Levels* — 45

Chapter 6 — Amanda's Meeting With Peter: *Common Reasons Why Coaching Fails* — 55

Chapter 7 — Lauren's Mentoring: *The Excellent Executive Coaching Process* — 65

Chapter 8 — Avoiding Common Coaching Mistakes: *Working With Brilliant and Abrasive Jerks* — 87

Chapter 9 — Coaching Is Systemic: *Keeping Management Aware and Accountable* — 109

Chapter 10 — Let the Client Lead: *Convincing an Abrasive Jerk to Start a Coaching Process* — 127

Chapter 11 — The Initial Triad Meeting: *A Balancing Act* — 143

Chapter 12 — Gathering Perceptions: *The Coworker Action Research Report* — 159

Chapter 13   Finding Patterns in the Feedback: *How the Coworker Action Research Report Works*   173

Chapter 14   Debriefing the Coworker Action Research Report: *The Coaching Starts*   189

Chapter 15   Integrating the Coaching Process: *Sustainable Change for the Abrasive Jerk and the Organization*   209

Epilogue: A Year Later   225
Appendix   227
Chapter Notes   237
About the Author   241

Acknowledgements

xi

This book is the result of a team effort. I extend my deepest gratitude to Laura Crawshaw. She has been a mentor to me with regard to coaching abrasive leaders. I have learned a tremendous amount from her with regard to these profiles.

I am grateful to Keri Menebroker for reading the manuscript and offering feedback. Thanks also to Rachel Fending for her encouragement and for doing a fabulous job editing the manuscript, to Patricia Porter for her support during the writing process, and, last but not least, to Laurens Bonnema for his outstanding illustrations.

Introduction

If you have worked for more than one boss in the course of your career, you are no doubt aware that not all leaders are the same. They differ wildly in the standards they set, the tone they take with their direct reports, the degree of involvement they prefer to have in minor decisions. Some bosses expect to be kept abreast of the most routine developments on a project; others view this level of detail as a waste of their time, trusting their employees to get the job done. Some bosses have after-work drinks with their employees and want to be considered as a friend; others are more standoffish, preferring to maintain a level of detachment. There are as many different types of leader as there are personalities, but research has grouped them into general categories of leadership style: for example, powerful and benevolent, inspirational, avoidant, demanding, authoritarian, and paternalistic.

Yet another group consists of leaders who are remarkably brilliant, charismatic, and driven—yet so abrasive on an interpersonal level that they become a liability to the company. Their enormous abilities might bring them success in the short term, but at the cost of long-term conflict and the eventual decline of their career. Such toxic leaders are often depicted as willfully destructive bullies or Machiavellian schemers.[1] Simply put, they're jerks.

An extensive body of research details the effects these leaders' behaviors have on their victims, colleagues who suffer their intolerance and insensitivity.[2] But what motivates abrasive leaders, and how they might be steered toward more positive ways of interacting with others, is less well understood.[3] The purpose of this book is to explore these questions, to shed light on the psychology of brilliant but abrasive leaders and what triggers their toxic behaviors.[i]

As an executive coach and founder and owner of both the Swiss coaching firm MKB Conseil & Coaching, Geneva, Switzerland, and of Excellent Executive Coaching, Las Vegas, USA, I have more than twenty years of experience working with leaders of major multinational organizations across Europe, Asia Pacific, and the Americas. In this book, I draw on that experience, particularly my work with brilliant but abrasive leaders, to share with you what motivates these individuals, how best to approach them when beginning a coaching process, and how to work with them to achieve deep, transformative change.

WORKPLACE AGGRESSION

The research on workplace satisfaction shows that companies lose a significant number of good employees each year because of poor leadership.[4] Addressing abrasive leadership can help organizations to retain talent, develop successors, avoid legal liability, reduce suffering in the workplace, and decrease employee turnover. In other words, it is *essential* for an organization's long-term sustainability.

Keeping employees engaged is key to improving an organization's performance.[5] Mismanagement of an organization, however, significantly reduces employee engagement. In an article in *Human Resource Management*, Marco Tavanti concluded that "toxic leaders' destructive behaviors and dysfunctional personal characteristics often generate enduring poisonous effects on those they lead. . . . They leave subordinates worse off than when they began."[6] This illustrates just one of the costs to organizations of allowing abrasive leadership to go unchecked.

---

i   The terms *toxic* and *abrasive behaviors* are used interchangeably throughout the book. Strictly defined, however, *toxic behavior* denotes harmful, poisonous relationships that inflict damage. Abrasive behavior, in contrast, annoys and frustrates people by wearing away at them and causes ill will.

THE CASE STUDY

Managing Brilliant and Abrasive Jerks is centered around a case study drawn from my own coaching experience (although fictionalized for anonymity's sake). At its heart is Peter Simmons, a visionary, action-oriented, highly successful executive whose blindness to the needs of his coworkers is jeopardizing his own success and the survival of his company. The book uses Peter's story as a jumping-off place from which to explore the mind of the abrasive jerk, what he or she fears and is driven by, and what spurs him or her to aggression.

As the story unfolds, you will also learn how skillful, effective coaching can help transform a toxic jerk into a positive asset for his or her organization and how to approach a resistant coaching client for the best chance of success. This is the story, both professionally insightful and personally inspiring, of an abrasive leader who ultimately becomes an example to those around him.

Peter Simmons is a decisive self-starter and problem solver who has rocketed up the corporate ladder at Tempus, a maker of fine watches in Switzerland. Nine months before this story begins, he was entrusted with the company's failing Asia division, which threatened to plunge the entire company into bankruptcy if it wasn't quickly reined in and made profitable. Two leaders before him had failed to rescue the division. Peter accepted the challenge and quickly got to the heart of the problem, cutting through corporate red tape to restructure the division. Now, under his leadership as executive vice president, the division is generating a growing stream of revenue.

Yet Peter is causing insidious costs to the company that the CEO, John Barbey, is unaware of. To everyone else, however, Peter's damaging rages are an open secret. As our story begins, Peter's colleagues and the company's board members have finally brought the problem to the CEO's attention. John Barbey has to recognize that although Peter has a high IQ, he is sadly lacking in emotional intelligence, or EQ. His behavior is causing suffering in the workplace and is destructive to the interests of the company.

Can anything be done to sustain Peter's productivity but change his abrasive leadership style? Is he capable of developing a more empowering approach to leadership? Can he transform from an abrasive jerk into a strong, effective leader? During the meeting with the company's CEO, the key stakeholders review their options and feel their way toward a solution.

Throughout the book, you will find resources to help you work more effectively with abrasive leaders, whether you are an executive coach, a human resources professional, a manager, or an employee with a difficult boss. As you read, you'll find detailed information on the flow of coaching sessions, sample correspondence to use with key stakeholders, and questions that encourage you to reflect on the issues presented in each chapter. My hope is that Peter's story will clarify for you the complex processes at work in the mind of an abrasive leader—and empower you to forge a productive and cooperative relationship with the abrasive jerks you encounter in your own professional life.

CAST OF CHARACTERS

Tempus's Executives

- Peter Simmons: Brilliant but abrasive jerk, executive vice president of the Asia division
- John Barbey: Chief executive officer
- George: Chief operating officer and Peter's boss
- Tom: Chief financial officer
- Gabrielle: Director of marketing
- Alex: Chief information officer

The Human Resources Department

- Frank: Director of human resources
- Lauren: Deputy human resources director and former professional coach
- Amanda: Human resources employee with some coaching experience

The Board of Directors

- Christopher, Jean, and Sonia: Members of the board

Chapter 1

Case Study

When Bright Leaders Become Abrasive Jerks

Corporate President John Barbey was worried. His fingers tapped in agitation on the arm of his large, brown leather chair. He stared out the window of his high-rise office in Geneva, Switzerland, turning over in his mind the questions he was facing. As president and CEO of Tempus, one of world's leading makers of fine watches, John was used to tackling complicated problems. This time, though, he felt torn.

Deep in thought, he watched the crowds bustling past, the splash of the fountains—and then his eye was caught by the *Broken Chair* sculpture erected across the square, in front of the United Nations building. The enormous sculpture stood almost as high as his office window: a simple wooden chair, like those found in dining rooms everywhere, except that one leg was missing, with only jagged splinters left where it had been torn away. The chair still stood, but it could no longer bear weight. The balance that kept it upright was delicate and could be upset with the slightest touch.

As he contemplated the sculpture, John realized that it perfectly symbolized the precarious position he was in. He felt he, too, was trying to keep his balance despite a missing limb.

John was worried by the continuous complaints he'd been hearing about one of his division heads, Peter Simmons—so worried, in fact, that he'd asked the key stakeholders to meet with him this afternoon to discuss the problem. Peter was John's protégé, and John had promoted him through the ranks of Tempus with lightning speed. After all, Peter had been given responsibility for the failing Asia division, which had been putting the entire company at risk of bankruptcy. He had accepted the challenge, and in record time he had restructured the division and brought it into solvency. Today, under Peter's leadership as executive vice president, the Asia division was generating a growing stream of revenue. Peter had proved to be extremely resourceful and had achieved outstanding results.

"So why all these complaints?" John wondered. A tap on the door interrupted his thoughts. The stakeholders he'd called together for a meeting had arrived: Frank, the senior human resources director, walked in first, followed by Alex, the company's chief information officer; Tom, the chief financial officer; and Gabrielle, the marketing director. Alex, Tom, and Gabrielle all worked closely with Peter Simmons and were his peers on the organizational chart.

A few board members—Christopher, Jean, and Sonia—ambled in after them. Finally, George, the chief operating officer and Peter Simmons's immediate boss, entered the room quietly and closed the door behind him. Once everybody had settled comfortably on the leather sofas in front of the CEO's massive desk, they looked at John expectantly and waited. John stiffened his back and looked at each of them in turn before interrupting the silence.

"As you know, I called you all here to talk about the complaints I've been hearing about Peter Simmons," John said. "Peter saved the Asia division from near bankruptcy and salvaged this company. Now I am supposed to believe he's causing chaos?"

For a moment, the group was silent. No one wanted to be the first to disappoint John. Then Alex blurted out, "The other day, Peter threatened to fire his deputy, Robert. Robert was presenting his project to my team, and Peter kept correcting him in front of everyone. He kept uttering comments like, 'That's such a stupid remark!' and swearing under his breath. Robert, who's usually an excellent speaker, started stuttering. He clearly felt completely undermined."

John nodded in acknowledgement. "I can see how that might feel humiliating."

Tom, the CFO, continued, "The problem is, we're losing good people. Valued employees have been leaving Peter's team for the last six months. And those who remain are beginning to feel stretched. Okay, so he's been responsible for a substantial increase in productivity. But now more and more work has to be done by fewer and fewer people. It's jeopardizing the quality provided by his division—and, consequently, mine."

"That's only part of the story," interrupted Frank, the head of human resources. "We've seen increased absenteeism and more stress-related illnesses since he arrived. Employees are regularly in my office complaining. They feel demoralized. Peter has socially isolated some of his direct reports. We're facing legal action for workplace bullying and discriminatory behavior."

"And he's just not interested in collaborative decision making," put in Gabrielle. "He constantly interrupts during brainstorming sessions to point out faulty logic in team members' reasoning, and he wants all the details to be mapped out for the long-term planning before we've had a chance to consider the options. My team just doesn't want to work with him."

"That sounds a bit unreasonable," John conceded. "I mean, I can imagine that Peter dominates meetings. He does have a commanding presence. And the sharp analytical skills he uses to solve complex business problems must help him detect the flaws in his peers' analysis."

"But it's more personal than that," Gabrielle interjected. "The other day, for example, I was chatting amicably with Peter while we were walking together to a meeting to present solutions for a failing consumer product. We discovered at the last minute that Julian, the corporate operating officer from worldwide operations, had come from headquarters and was joining us. At one point, Julian stopped my presentation to ask a few questions.

"Before I had a chance to speak, Peter interrupted and proceeded to rip apart all my suggestions. He pitted me against Tom, the marketing department against finance, playing us against each other and exposing contradictions in our arguments.

"I know Peter can be very charming and service oriented with clients, but he takes advantage of confidential information to gossip and undermine our authority. In front of Julian, he made me look incompetent and unprepared. I thought we were all working for the same company!"

"Exactly!" George said. "The tension he's creating between me and my peers is trickling down and making cross-silo projects practically impossible to implement. It's causing infighting among our divisions, as well as turf protection. He's not a team player. It's intolerable!"

Brilliant but abrasive jerks often pit people against each other and inhibit creative thinking.

Gabrielle looked pleadingly at John Barbey, silently urging him to take action. Tom spoke up. "You see the problem, John? Peter's behavior is counterproductive and detrimental to a collegial work environment."

Frank nodded in agreement. "And there's a human cost to all this. Peter's habit of isolating and humiliating people he doesn't care for incites them to retaliatory responses. Employees are spending unproductive time discussing how to get back at him, not to mention having to clean up the emotional mess after meetings with other divisions.

"I've been told that many of his meetings are essentially monologues. No one dares speak up. What a missed opportunity to use the creative minds on his team. And there's more absenteeism than ever before—some of his direct reports dread dealing with him so much that they are calling in sick."

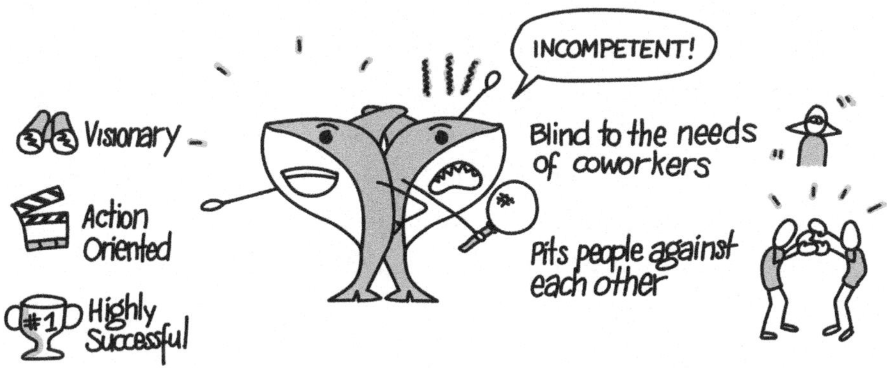

Finding himself outnumbered and hoping for support, John turned to Peter Simmons's functional boss. "What do you make of all this, George?"

"Well, I have to say, I agree. He seems to go out of his way to antagonize me in public. He's impatient when I question him, and I know he criticizes my decisions as soon as my back's turned. I've heard some of the things he says about me, and they're not flattering. I'm told he calls me a bozo behind my back. To be perfectly honest, I think he's a jerk."

John reflected on what he'd heard and was puzzled. Peter had always struck him as so charismatic and persuasive. John was surprised by such seething, visible frustration among crucial members of his management team. With John, Peter Simmons was docile, almost servile, like a son who goes to great lengths to please his father.

John knew Peter was a fast thinker, and his rapid processing sometimes prevented him from listening to others. And it was true that Peter seemed to always have an opinion about everything and might come across as a know-it-all. That being said, he usually *did* have the answers.

John knew Peter was a self-made man. His immigrant parents operated a small watch store, and Peter went to Harvard on a scholarship, after graduating as valedictorian of his high school class. He was incredibly driven and had an incisive, logical mind. His impatience with people who weren't as quick as he was caused him to sometimes miss subtle but important details. Often, he had no equally intelligent counterpart in meetings to question his quick, sharp assumptions. It left his colleagues at a loss.

Peter took extraordinarily high levels of performance for granted, both for himself and for others. He was always on call at any time of day or night and expected no less of his direct reports and colleagues. They complained that Peter's phone calls frequently interrupted family dinners. If the week's work was behind schedule, he regularly asked his direct reports to come in on Sunday morning to finish a project. More than a few weekend family trips had been canceled at the last minute after an "emergency" call from Peter.

Brilliant but abrasive leaders tend to be highly ambitious and driven. They hold themselves to an extremely high performance standard and expect the same from their coworkers.

Some people thought of Peter as a visionary for his ideas about what his division could become, but to others he just seemed delusional. He obtained excellent results, but at what cost? Even John couldn't deny that he had overheard Peter ranting in the hallway that work–life balance was for the weak and the lethargic. However, Peter was exceptionally charming and persuasive with clients. And he closed deals that even his boss, George, might have had difficulty with.

Frank broke into John's thoughts with another diatribe. "If Peter perceives a direct report as displaying disloyalty, he retaliates by publicly humiliating or ostracizing that person. Six of his direct reports have recently quit or asked to be transferred to other divisions.

"Only yesterday, Janine was crying in my office. She works twelve hours a day, but every time she submits a report to Peter, he skims quickly through it and then tears it apart. When she starts explaining, he waves her away, tapping on his keyboard to avoid eye contact or out of sheer boredom. He never suggests improvements—he thinks she is hopeless. He completely rewrote the last report she handed in, which made her feel totally useless. When I told Peter that Janine was thinking of leaving his division, he answered, 'Good riddance! She's incompetent.'

"The other day, I had to spend an hour coaxing a young trainee not to quit because he'd said to her, 'Hey, pretty girl, late again? Did you have another hot date last night?' The only direct reports he favors are exceptionally quick and totally devoted to him."

"So you think he's jeopardizing the continuity of the division long term?" John asked.

"No! No!" interrupted Jean, one of the board members. "It sounds like he's getting rid of the least competent employees and keeping the best and most able. This company has a collegial work ethic, but we also demand high standards."

"That's one way of looking at it," said Christopher, another board member. "He simply doesn't accept mediocre performance. Peter is obviously retaining the brightest stars, but if he doesn't tolerate any contradiction, isn't he just surrounding himself with yes men? If he doesn't let people think for themselves, how can he develop a successor?"

John could sense that three of his division heads wanted him to take action against Peter Simmons and have him fired. John wanted to protect Peter and give him every opportunity for continued success, even though he was beginning to see the counter effects of Peter's high performance. Was Peter really abrasive, or just demanding? Were the other division heads jealous of Peter's success? Surely this was a temporary problem caused by the challenge of turning around the Asia division?

The conversation called to John's mind an article on "brilliant and abrasive jerks" that he had read recently. According to the author, Dr. Katrina Burrus, these individuals are high-achieving, driven leaders who have a high IQ but low emotional intelligence (or EQ). They tend to disregard other people's emotions in the interest of obtaining results—which reduces their effectiveness at the individual, team, and organizational levels.

Yes, this sounded like Peter, but John felt torn. Even though Peter's behavior was detrimental and counterproductive to a collegial work environment, he *had* turned around his division where others had failed.

John was jolted out of his reverie when George stood up and said, with uncharacteristic force, "Fire him now. You'll have to do it sooner or later. No one dares propose ideas anymore for fear of being blasted with insults. Six of his direct reports have already left the company, slamming the door behind them. How many more need to leave before we take action?"

"No, don't fire him!" interrupted Jean. "If you hurt him, he'll lose his momentum. He's still immature as a leader, but his roughness will iron itself out. My guess is that when he's been in his current position longer, he'll relax and be less aggressive. Why do you care, anyway? He's making money for the company, and he turned around his division when no one else could."

"He's going through a divorce," Christopher explained. "It's a temporary situation. Turning around a division is no easy task. Aren't we all abrasive in moments of stress? In fact, my wife accused me of being a jerk only this morning!"

Jean chimed in, "We could transfer him to another division that needs a turnaround."

While everyone in the room was competing to get his attention, John reflected on the article by Dr. Burrus. Peter Simmons was clearly abrasive—but oh, so brilliant. Still undecided about how to handle the situation, John thought it might be the right time to call in an expert.

Lauren Schultz, the company's recently hired HR deputy, was a specialist in interpersonal relations. Before coming to the company, she had been an executive coach at MKB Excellent Executive Coaching, specialists in coaching brilliant and abrasive leaders and executives of large, global organizations. John thought she might be just the person to help him navigate this thorny issue.

Chapter Review Questions

1. How is an abrasive leader defined?
2. What has Peter Simmons done or said that defines him as an abrasive leader?
3. What are an abrasive jerk's costs to the company, teams, and individuals? How does Peter Simmons impact the company, both negatively and positively?
4. What excuses do the board members offer for Peter's behavior?

CHAPTER 2

BRILLIANT JERKS' DNA

Who Are They? How Can They Be Identified?

Most people have come into contact with a bright but abrasive leader at some point in their professional life, often without even realizing it. The demanding boss who expected you to work weekends to complete a project but was never pleased with the results, the department head who led his team to record-setting performance levels but whose unpredictable outbursts terrified everyone he worked with, the executive who spread rumors and undermined anyone who threatened to outperform her—all these are examples of bright but abrasive leaders.

A brilliant but abrasive leader is any manager or leader who is extremely talented but is driven to gain recognition above all else. They are exceptionally intelligent, but they use that intelligence for their own professional benefit rather than in the best interest of the company. Moreover, they are blinded to the costs their behavior has for individuals, teams, and the organization as a whole.

This incivility, however, is not generalized or constant. On the contrary, abrasive leaders can be incredibly charismatic. When not under pressure, they tend to be winning, funny, and engaging, and they are very good at bringing these traits to bear in a professional context. They have an almost mesmerizing charm with clients and, due to their razor-sharp intelligence, strong powers of persuasion.

When their professional reputation is at stake, however, abrasive leaders show another side entirely. They are remarkably driven, focused on success and on being regarded as highly—even uniquely—competent. They work tirelessly and expect the same of their direct reports. If they perceive a threat to their competence, they will do whatever it takes to squash it.

A perceived threat to their professional reputation or self-image will send brilliant but abrasive jerks into attack mode immediately.

They may berate employees who fail to meet unreasonable deadlines, fly into screaming rages, even physically threaten coworkers. They undermine employees by creating conflict, withholding critical resources, and abruptly changing deadlines. They wage a kind of "psychological warfare" against colleagues they perceive as posing a threat: ignoring or ridiculing a coworker's contributions, constantly mocking and belittling a coworker, using confidential information about a coworker to spread rumors, or deliberately excluding a coworker from important meetings and social activities. They may give discriminatorily negative performance appraisals, intentionally fail to acknowledge good work, or micromanage an employee to an extent that makes work impossible.

Needless to say, this behavior has a significant negative impact, not just on the targeted employees but on the organization as a whole. Abrasive leaders can destroy people's self-confidence and inflict serious, lasting damage. They create a culture of fear that robs employees of their voice in the organization and deadens creativity. This toxic environment erodes morale and causes turnover to spike, so that it becomes hard to retain the company's best talent.

A closer look at our case study gives a clear picture of the makeup of the brilliant and abrasive leader, as well as what motivates him or her to behave in such a destructive manner.

CASE STUDY: WHAT IS AN ABRASIVE LEADER?

Several minutes after John put down the phone, there was a light knock, and Lauren Schultz put her head around the door, an engaging smile on her face. As the group took seats at the conference table, John filled

Lauren in on the problems people were having with Peter Simmons. He mentioned that he'd recently read an article about bright but abrasive leaders and felt Peter might fit the type.

"Can you help us understand a bit more about this kind of leader?" he asked Lauren.

Lauren smiled. "I'd be happy to," she said. "First of all, abrasive leaders' behaviors have an important influence on employees. Second, these leaders' toxic or abrasive behaviors put a great deal of stress on employees, which has long-term effects on the company's output and productivity. Before we come to Peter's case, I'm wondering, have any of you been in contact with abrasive leaders before? What have you noticed regarding their behavior?"

Gabrielle, the company's marketing director, spoke up. "Many years ago, I worked as an executive secretary to an abrasive boss. Her temper was explosive, and it could be triggered by small issues as well as important ones. Her anger wasn't only directed toward me. In fact, I was the one who usually escaped her tantrums. Her direct reports were totally intimidated, though. They were afraid to talk to her or share information."

"I want to underline two points that you just mentioned," said Lauren. "First of all, your boss caused fear in people. Second, people began to avoid giving her updates. What other behavior did she show?"

Gabrielle thought for a moment, then said, "She didn't get negative information early enough to correct a problem, because people were afraid to tell her. So she often didn't learn what needed fixing until it was too late and became a crisis."

"Can you go into a bit more detail about this?" Lauren asked. "What did she specifically say or do?"

"Well," said Gabrielle, "whenever an employee informed her of a missed deadline or if a report wasn't done properly, she would fly into a rage. She would bang her fist on the desk and rant at the person for being a lazy, incompetent idiot. She threatened to fire people. Most of her direct reports took the beatings submissively because they had families to support. I hated listening to these tirades, though. I would usually escape to the restroom because my heart was beating too fast and my hands were sweaty."

"So she was accusatory in an emotional and explosive fashion," reflected Lauren. "She threatened her direct reports. Would you say that she took her anger out on whoever was nearest to hand—shooting the messenger, perhaps?"

"Your description is spot on!" Gabrielle exclaimed.

"Good," said Lauren. "I think we're starting to develop a picture of the bright but abrasive leader type. Has anyone else had experience with a person like this?"

Sonia spoke up next. "I worked with a former hockey player who was the CFO of a razor blade company," she related. "When he was angry, he would come raging at you, towering over you, pointing his finger in your face. I would cringe and feel like a two-year-old being scolded by her father. He was so physically imposing and got so angry, I was afraid he might lose control altogether and hit me, though he never did.

"He blew events out of proportion. I was the finance director, and he would withhold critical information from me so I could not do my job properly, then humiliate me in meetings. It seems that Gabrielle and I had the same type of boss."

"You've just described several abrasive behaviors," observed Lauren. "First, your boss used his physical presence to intimidate you and underscore verbal attacks. This is similar to the way animals behave when they feel threatened. Birds ruffle up their feathers and cats raise their hair on end, to appear bigger and frighten their opponent into withdrawal. Your boss also gave incomplete requests and withheld critical information to impede you from doing your work correctly. What triggered this behavior?"

Many abrasive leaders use their physical presence to intimidate people.

Sonia grimaced. "If people didn't do what he said according to his timeline, or if coworkers didn't perform as well as he could have, it would set him off. Sometimes his anger was caused by something that happened before he came to work, and he would start the day by screaming at everyone. Why do people like this behave so destructively?"

How Is the Abrasive Leader Defined?

In my experience coaching abrasive leaders, I have found that they have terrible blind spots. They lack what Daniel Goleman termed *emotional intelligence* (otherwise known as EQ), the ability to monitor and manage one's own emotions and to read and effectively respond to the emotions and motivations of others.[i] They lack empathy. They place enormous focus and importance on results, but they fail to see that to increase results, they need to engage autonomous, thinking, creative people who are not submissive to their leader's every request.

In their obsession with what they need to achieve, abrasive leaders often fail to recognize the importance of keeping people positively engaged. Many are perfectionists, never satisfied with their own work and continually pushing themselves to work harder, raise the bar, accomplish more. Intensely motivated to gain recognition through outstanding results, they expect no less of the people around them and can be very hard on their employees. At best, they put constant pressure on their direct reports and offer little to no recognition. At worst, they isolate, castigate, or humiliate them.

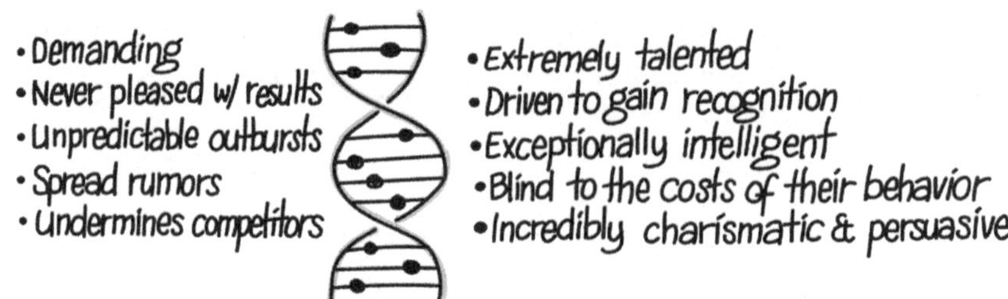

---

i   *EQ* is the common abbreviation for *emotional quotient,* a (notional) measure of a person's adequacy in such areas as self-awareness, empathy, and sensitive interactions with other people. (Daniel Goleman, *Emotional Intelligence.* New York: Bantam Books, 1995.)

In the case study above, Sonia raised the question of why abrasive leaders behave so destructively. Don't they realize the harm their bullying does? It's important to understand that these leaders have a blind spot: their understanding of other people's emotions. Leaders of this type are not naturally tuned in to what others are thinking and feeling; their focus is on goals and outcomes rather than on people. They lack empathy and self-awareness—that is, they have low emotional intelligence.

Because they are not good at reading others' emotions, abrasive leaders often find it difficult to maintain positive interpersonal relationships. They can hurt people without intending to. Some abrasive leaders are good at identifying people's weaknesses, which requires interpersonal insight, but they use this skill to satisfy their drive toward perfectionism and, by doing so, harm and manipulate people. Abrasive leaders' lack of EQ and their underlying anxiety often translate into explosive and uncontrolled emotional outbursts that provide them with only temporary relief. In many cases, they don't have the empathy to realize the harm they have done.

Characteristics of an Abrasive Jerk

- Causes workplace division and conflict instead of harmony
- Undermines or sabotages others
- Exhibits poor self-control and restraint
- Is physically threatening or engages in psychological bullying
- Yells, screams, is sarcastic or otherwise verbally abusive
- Shows callousness and lack of empathy
- Has shallow emotional affect—genuine emotion is short-lived and egocentric
- Shows signs of perfectionism
- Micromanages
- Sets unrealistic standards and changes deadlines without notice or reason
- Has mesmerizing charm and strong powers of persuasion

- Is extremely competitive with other employees
- Has a grandiose sense of self-worth
- Fails to accept responsibility for actions
- Exhibits a manipulative, cunning, and often discriminatory attitude (e.g., sexism)
- Gossips or spreads rumors about coworkers
- Uses private or confidential information to denigrate a coworker
- Continuously gives excessive amounts of work to an employee
- Ignores, ridicules, or belittles a coworker's contributions
- Purposely fails to acknowledge good work
- Gives discriminatorily negative performance appraisals
- Shows favoritism or treats some coworker differently than others

---

ABRASIVE LEADERS' FEAR OF FAILURE

Additionally, abrasive leaders are often defensive and on high alert for challenges to their leadership. They feel personally threatened by their direct reports' failures, such as when deadlines are not met. To protect themselves, they feel a strong need to control their environment. An unpredictable environment causes them anxiety, and their sharp, logical mind runs ahead of them, rooting out signs of failure in themselves and others. Once this anxiety is released, the abrasive leader may feel remorse but be unsure how to control these outbursts of anger.

* * *

As Lauren detailed the characteristics of the brilliant but abrasive jerk, the others gathered in the room nodded in understanding. They recognized not just Peter in her description, but other people they had worked with over the years, as well.

"I used to serve on the board of directors for a company with a CEO who might have been an abrasive leader," said Christopher. "I remember a meeting when she was making an important presentation to the board of directors. In the middle of the presentation, she realized that one of her essential papers was missing.

"This was a critical meeting for her—if she didn't win board approval of her plans, her project would be cancelled. She excused herself from the board room for a minute and rushed out to her office, and we could hear her screaming at the top of her lungs to her deputy. Her deputy stared at her in fear, started trembling, then ran out of the office.

"Rationally, if the CEO wanted her deputy to find the paper as quickly as possible, she shouldn't have reduced him to a state of terror. So what happened? Why such an outburst from an exceptionally intelligent woman?"

"It is likely she was not thinking about how her behavior affected her deputy," explained Lauren. "She was too engrossed in her own fears. The prospect of her presentation failing in front of the board of directors terrified her. Brilliant but abrasive leaders are not equipped to handle fear of failure. Your CEO coped by exploding and framing the catastrophe as her deputy's fault, of course, not hers."

Christopher was incredulous. "How is it possible that she had no idea of the impact her behavior had on her deputy?"

"Her emotional outburst was an expression of anxiety and a reaction to the threat of failure to win approval for her project," Lauren said. "She might also have believed that through intimidation, she could jolt her coworkers into being more competent. Your CEO likely had a win–lose mind-set focused on staying dominant in the corporate pecking order and would attack anything that got in her way. At the board meeting, her anxiety was triggered by the threat that she might not perform to her own expectations."

"That makes sense," said Christopher.

"But Gabrielle also gave us an example of a leader who was faced with unpredictable change," continued Lauren, "and that provoked a similar anxiety reaction. Abrasive leaders' outbursts are caused by anxiety, but the exterior triggers that cause the outburst can differ. In the cases we've talked about, one was the threat of being perceived as incompetent, and the other was the threat of unpredictability. So we have now identified some of the characteristics of abrasive leaders."

*   *   *

Lauren's explanation in the case study has painted a clear picture of the abrasive jerk. But is it possible to motivate employees and achieve impressive results without being abrasive? What is the difference between an abrasive leader and a demanding one? In the next chapter, we'll explore those questions in depth, as Lauren continues her discussion with the group in John's office.

Chapter Review Questions

1. What are five characteristics of a brilliant but abrasive jerk?
2. What are some examples of abrasive leadership?
3. What leadership qualities does Peter Simmons lack? What is his blind spot?
4. What does Peter fear?

CHAPTER 3

WHAT DOES IT TAKE TO BE A SUCCESSFUL LEADER?

The Key Differences Between Abrasive and Demanding Leaders

The abrasive leadership style often succeeds in getting results from employees. Under pressure, they tend to rise to the challenge and deliver well. To the untrained eye, this might look like an effective, if unpleasant, means of motivating people. So what distinguishes an abrasive leader from a demanding leader? Is there even a difference?

DEMANDING VERSUS ABRASIVE LEADERSHIP

Of course, the answer is yes, there *is* a difference. Once you know what to look for, it's fairly easy to tell these two types of leaders apart. A demanding boss and an abrasive boss both seek high performance and challenge their direct reports to deliver. However, they approach this task in completely different ways. A demanding boss tries to understand what his or her employees need to perform at peak level, and supports them with resources and information when they are handling difficult tasks. The demanding boss has high expectations and confidence in the employee's ability to succeed.

If the direct report fails, the demanding boss analyzes whether the direct report was *unable* or *unwilling* to complete the assigned task, and reacts accordingly.[i] If the person put his or her best efforts into achieving the goal but was simply unsuccessful, the leader provides support or education to help the direct report do his or her job better. If the employee was unwilling to put in the necessary effort, then the boss changes his or her management style or has a serious, honest conversation with the employee to get to the heart of the matter.

---

i   Ken Blanchard's Situational Leadership II Model uses the terms *competence* (i.e., ability, knowledge, and skill) and *commitment* (i.e., confidence and motivation) to describe different levels of employee development. For more on Blanchard's model, see http://www.kenblanchard.com.

Conversely, the abrasive leader, when confronted with a direct report who has failed, tends to damage that employee's self-confidence. Abrasive leaders perceive the failure of direct reports as reflecting on their own leadership and abilities and, therefore, as a serious threat. Accordingly, they respond with anger. Employees don't get enough support to resolve issues, and they are left feeling disempowered, depressed, and confused about what to do. Let's turn back to our case study for a closer look at the differences between these two types of leaders.

*　＊　＊*

As Lauren described to the assembled group the specific characteristics of each leadership style, there were scattered nods of recognition and understanding. It was becoming clear to the group that there was, in fact, a critical difference between abrasive and demanding leadership.

"Over a long time," observed Tom, "the abrasive leader can wear away your soul."

"A demanding boss provides enough specific, detailed feedback so that the employee knows exactly what action to take in order to improve," said Lauren. "This releases some of the tension caused by the employee's failure to perform to the desired level and meet the set challenges, in a way that is motivational—or at least not destructive."

Alex, the company's chief information officer, observed, "A demanding leader leaves you feeling challenged and excited."

"The demanding boss attacks the problem, and the abrasive boss attacks the person," said Christopher.

Gabrielle agreed. "Yes! When I worked with an abrasive boss, my husband used to say that I came back from work a few inches shorter each day. He did wear away my soul. I felt worthless."

KEY DIFFERENCES BETWEEN DEMANDING AND ABRASIVE LEADERS

Demanding Leader	Abrasive Leader
Stretches employees to develop their competencies. Leads employees out of their comfort zone and into their stretch zone, but is careful not to overstretch an employee without providing support, resources, and a show of belief in the person. Monitors the stress inflicted on employees.	Demands results, and overlooks the difficulties employees might have encountered and the significant effort they might have exerted to reach their objectives. Lacks faith in employees' capacity, and makes it known.
Observes and analyzes the causes of the problem. Communicates high but achievable expectations. Takes into account the competencies of each individual or team. Confers tools, support, or mentoring to enhance employees' success and self-confidence.	Assumes too quickly that a lack of results is due to employees' laziness or stupidity. Does not identify the developmental potential of each individual. Does not notice when employees are willing but lack the competencies to accomplish the task.
Supports employees when they are confronted with a problem.	Blames, criticizes, or humiliates employees who do not reach their objectives.
Takes into consideration coworkers' efforts. Does not focus only on the results.	Criticizes employees who fail to achieve results, even when they worked night and day to meet the set goal. Focuses primarily on results.
Focuses on employees' positive contribution and addresses the areas where they need improvement.	Focuses on the employee's errors. Renders the employee defensive.
Realizes when a coworker has difficulties with tasks that the leader finds easy to do.	Is unaware that what is easy for him or her might be difficult for others. Has unconscious competencies (i.e., takes his or her talents for granted and expects others to have the same capabilities).
Does not feel psychologically threatened or incompetent if coworkers do not achieve their goals.	Feels threatened by employees' lack of competence and failure to produce results in a timely manner.
Uses a repertoire of leadership styles to motivate direct reports, and considers the context in which results should be achieved.	Does not adapt to the person and context. Has a limited leadership repertoire when reacting to a stressful situation.
Motivates coworkers through feedback.	Gives feedback that makes coworkers feel depressed and incompetent.
Makes people feel challenged but respected.	Makes people feel pushed to their limits. Often causes people to feel exploited, which creates resentment and passive resistance.

*   *   *

Now that we have identified the differences between a demanding leader and an abrasive one, let's review when and why a difficult leader may react abrasively. These leaders are not consistently abrasive, which makes them all the more unpredictable and destabilizing. At MKB Excellent Executive Coaching, I have coached abrasive leaders who were charming and witty. Their clients found them to be agreeable, humorous, and extremely client-oriented.

In our particular case study, the combination of Peter's intelligence, his charisma, and his persuasive skills allows him to close deals with clients when others might have failed. Peter can be outstandingly charming and persuasive. He is not systematically aggressive toward people. Rather, he seems to alternate between open friendliness and malice or even rage. People may feel like they are dealing with Dr. Jekyll and Mr. Hyde, never knowing what might set him off on a tirade.[ii]

Jekyll & Hyde

Faced with an abrasive leader, employees learn to walk on tiptoe until they can gauge his or her mood. Such unpredictable behavior is perhaps even more unsettling than consistent nastiness, because employees find it difficult to predict the reaction they will get at any given time. To understand better when and why abrasive leaders feel threatened and why they may react by attacking their opponent, we can draw a parallel with behaviors found in the animal world.

COMPARING THE ABRASIVE JERK'S BEHAVIORS TO THE ANIMAL WORLD

When faced with a threat, animals respond in one of three ways: fight, flight, or freezing.[1] If an antelope's territory is threatened by a trespassing

---

ii   This unpredictability is an important attribute that is discussed further in the chapters on coaching the abrasive leader (in particular, Chapters 7 and 8).

buck from another herd, the animal will likely choose to fight to defend its boundary and repel the intruder. If the antelope encounters a lion on the hunt, however, it will react quite differently. Now it is in a predator–prey situation. Perceiving a threat to its life and little chance of winning a fight, the antelope will choose flight and run away as fast as possible. If the antelope is caught by surprise face to face with the predator, though, it might simply freeze, too petrified to take action. Freezing is a common reaction among animals that feel trapped. This response does not offer any physical release of tension, as do fighting and fleeing.

Now let us make a parallel with the abrasive leader. In the case study, we learned that Peter threatened to fire his deputy, Robert, for bungling a presentation. Within the scope of professional life, losing one's job is analogous to being killed, and therefore is extremely anxiety provoking.[2] Peter in this case is like the animal whose territory is threatened: He is ready to fight off the trespasser. The flight-or-fight response is meant to be a temporary physical reaction to help an animal or person escape a danger-ous situation. If this anxiety-provoking situation lasts over time, however, the prolonged stress can cause physical illness.[3]

* * *

In the conference room, Lauren detailed the three threat responses in the animal kingdom, describing their analogy to the professional world. "What behavioral strategy was Peter using when he constantly cor-rected Robert's presentation in front of everyone and called his remarks stupid?" she asked the group.

"He was in fight mode," Alex answered.

"You're right, Alex. Peter was not only humiliating Robert but also impeding him from concentrating on his presentation. Robert's distress was visible when he started stuttering. Robert had at least three possible ways of reacting to Peter Simmons. Which reaction did he choose?"

"I'm not sure," said Tom.

Lauren explained to the group, "Robert could have fought back, at the risk of a public outburst from Peter. He also could have packed up his papers and escaped from the presentation without saying a word, had he opted for the flight strategy. Instead, he froze. Robert, an intelligent and eloquent man, was literally incapacitated by his stuttering and unable to continue his presentation. As with fights between animals, Peter asserted his dominance and superiority by belittling Robert as inferior in the pecking order, and Robert froze, petrified.

"We know that Peter attacked Robert because he felt threatened," continued Lauren. "But what *caused* him to feel threatened? There are two likely reasons for Peter's wrath. It's possible that Robert was doing a poor job on the presentation, and Peter felt it could negatively reflect on his own leadership competence. Alternatively, if Peter felt that Robert was giving an excellent presentation, he might have perceived a threat to his authority, a potential new 'head of the pack.' If that were the case, he would have felt compelled to prove he was more capable than Robert."

"When Peter shows tactless behavior," spoke up Frank, "I have seen people go into total shutdown mode. They freeze. Some people have complained of being demotivated and asked me to transfer them to another division, which I guess is the flight reaction. By moving divisions, they are, in effect, retreating. In the organizational world, employees could also retreat by avoiding interactions with their boss as much as possible. I guess not giving your abrasive leader information is also a flight strategy."

"Exactly, Frank," concurred Lauren. "It might also be a form of passive resistance, an undercover fight mode. Let's remember that a behavior strategy is not permanent or fixed. We can use any one of these strategies several times a day, according to the context or person we are confronted with. Sometimes flight mode is the best strategy to avoid destructive and unnecessary arguments. But what do you think is the abrasive leader's preferred behavioral strategy—fight, flight, or freezing?"

"Fight, of course," replied Frank.

"Yes, it usually is. Abrasive leaders attack when they want to move higher in the pecking order. They attack when a colleague makes them feel incompetent or when they perceive a threat to their status. What specifically threatens them at any particular time can vary, but it is most often insecurity about their competence. This is counterintuitive, because most abrasive leaders are high achievers, perfectionists, and results oriented, but any perceived threat to their status could provoke an uncontrolled reaction. The outburst provides release from the perceived threat.

"However," Lauren continued, "how would you explain why Peter is so servile with John? If we are to continue comparing human behavior to behavior in the animal kingdom, how do you think Peter views you, Mr. Barbey? As a predator, or as prey?"

"As his boss, I guess I fill the role of a predator," said John.

"Yes, he sees you as a predator who is more powerful than he is. You mentioned that he is continually seeking your approval. How does he view George, who's his immediate boss?"

Lauren paused, looked at George, and hesitated before continuing. "Sorry, George, but he might be perceiving you mostly as prey, which is the reason why he attacks you. Calling you names and gossiping about you behind your back undermines your authority. He is competing with you, and he probably feels he can do better than you—or at least he wants to *think* he can. This is also a form of passive aggression."

"So Peter sees John as a predator," said Frank, "and his preferred strategy with John is to use the flight mode if they are in disagreement. Since Peter perceives George as prey, he feels he can win the battle by using the fight strategy, either directly or surreptitiously. That makes sense."

"If Peter's behavior is abnormally abrasive when he's under stress, then he might feel easily threatened and resort to defensive behavior, such as fight or flight, or freeze at the perceived threat to his self-image," added Lauren.

"Does Peter really feel vulnerable?" Jean asked. "He seems so confident."

"And why is he also aggressive with direct reports who are no threat to him?" put in Frank.

Lauren answered, "Peter is intellectually brilliant, and he is impatient and irritated by people who are 'slower' than he is. He lacks the insight to see that it might be challenging for others to do what is so easy for him. He does not have the empathy to understand the distress his behavior causes. He has unconscious competencies—that is, he takes his extraordinary abilities for granted as standard issue—and assumes that if his direct reports are not doing their work correctly, they are lazy (i.e., unwilling) or stupid (i.e., unable)."

The group assembled around the conference table nodded in understanding.

"For example," Lauren continued, "when Janine gave Peter a report that was not to his liking, he categorized her immediately as incompetent. Again, Peter's unconscious competence leads him to assume work that comes easily to him will be easy for Janine, as well. This sort of assumption is not unusual among brilliant leaders.

"Additionally, any failure on Janine's part is perceived as a direct threat to Peter's success. She works for him, and he is afraid that her difficulties and lack of competence are a reflection on him. If he thinks she is unwilling to do the job, then he will interpret this resistance as insubordination. And what will his reaction be, fight or flight?"

Frank replied, "Okay, so when Peter perceives something as insubordination, he will take the fight approach and attack."

"He feels psychologically threatened by Janine's lack of results," added Gabrielle. "He projects his own fear of failure onto other people who are not succeeding according to his criteria."

Sonia offered, "Abrasive leaders can't attack themselves or accept their limitations, so they attack other people?"

"Why don't all bosses act this way?" asked Jean.

"I'm not a psychologist," answered Lauren, "but my assumption is that brilliant but abrasive leaders have a strong drive to perform, and they feel they are only as good as the results they achieve. If they fail, they feel worthless and unloved, and they start doubting themselves."

"This is getting too psychological for me," Tom objected. "Let's get back to Peter."

"Okay," said Lauren, "let's take the opposite situation. Let's say Peter perceives a coworker as more competent than he is. In this case, he will accept the colleague's skill, as long as he receives credit for the results he has achieved. It's also important that the competent individual does not pose any threat to Peter's leadership and helps Peter obtain better results."

Brilliant but abrasive leaders display the same instinctive responses as animals: when they feel threatened, they attack.

"But the abrasive leaders I have worked with seem to respect a person who tells them off when they behave badly," said Gabrielle. "How can you explain that?"

Lauren replied, "Often, abrasive leaders respect coworkers who stand up to them gently but firmly. They have a regard for people who set boundaries around acceptable behavior. Sometimes, an abrasive leader may view a person who states his or her position in a quiet but firm way as rising in the pecking order."

* * *

This behavior is similar to how a wolf might respond to the pack's alpha male. Abrasive leaders need to feel that their superiors are intelligent, capable, and effective. When that is the case, they will respect their superiors' authority and behave with deference. Peter's relationship with John is a good example.

Regardless of whether the abrasive leader is dealing with a superior or someone lower on the organizational chart, the leader needs to be perceived as competent. Anything that endangers his or her image as a skilled, capable leader who is thoroughly in control will trigger some form of attack. Fast and Chen found, across four separate studies, that people in a position of power become aggressive when they feel their power being threatened by what they see as their own inadequacies.[4] The authors referred to this phenomenon as *ego threat* and found that it was diminished when participants received feedback that increased their sense of self-worth.

Abrasive leaders have a strong drive to perform, and they feel they are only as good as the results they achieve. Perceived failures threaten their sense of self-worth, and they may lash out in defense.

Take the example of the CEO who could not find the papers she crucially needed for the board meeting. She wanted to be seen as competent and show that she was doing a good job. When she asked her deputy to get her the papers and saw that he couldn't locate them immediately, she perceived him as a threat. He was not giving her what she needed quickly enough for her to look good in the eyes of the board members, so she attacked him. She used an outburst of anger at her deputy as a way to release her anxiety and deal with the threat that she could be perceived as incompetent. She very likely did so without pausing to think or weigh the wisdom of her outburst; she was simply acting out her anxiety. Her amygdala was activating adrenaline throughout her body against a perceived threat. Her reaction was unconscious and immediate, like snatching one's hand away from a hot stove burner.

Brilliant but abrasive leaders may seem to behave counterintuitively or even illogically as they attempt to achieve their goals, but it's important to bear in mind that their actions are very likely instinctive, taken without conscious thought. This counters the belief that abrasive jerks are consciously manipulative. In the next chapter, we'll turn back to our case study to delve into the effects abrasive jerks' behaviors can have on coworkers, teams, and the organization as a whole.

Chapter Review Questions

1. In what ways are the abrasive leader's reactions to threat similar to responses in the animal kingdom?
2. Describe a leader's flight, fight, and freeze reactions to a threat in an organization.
3. What is the abrasive leader's motivation to excel?
4. How is an abrasive leader distinguished from a demanding boss? Is Peter abrasive or simply demanding?
5. When giving feedback, what does the brilliant and abrasive leader focus on, and what does the demanding boss focus on?

CHAPTER 4

TOXIC BEHAVIOR IS A VIRUS

What Are the Abrasive Jerk's Insidious Effects on Individuals, Teams, and Organizations?

Toxic behavior in the workplace has a trickle-down effect that spreads throughout the bully's division and eventually, if left unchecked, across the whole organization. In fact, workplace bullying is so damaging that many organizations have a policy in place to prevent it. *Workplace bullying* is commonly defined as "persistent, offensive, abusive, intimidating or insulting behavior or unfair actions directed at another individual, causing the recipient to feel threatened, abused, humiliated or vulnerable."[1] This certainly sounds like the brilliant but abrasive leader!

Abrasive jerks tend to be adept at manipulating social interactions to protect their own interests; they use ostracism, discrimination, and favoritism to shift the social balance in their favor. These tactics sow jealousy, anger, and resentment among colleagues and can, over time, effectively redraw the map of interpersonal relations in an organization. When an abrasive leader perceives an employee to be a threat, he or she may try to isolate that person or drive a wedge between the person and his or her colleagues, much as a wolf separates its chosen prey from the pack (for more on ways abrasive leaders' behavior parallels animals' instinctive responses, see Chapter 3). The abrasive leader might intentionally exclude certain coworkers from meetings that are critical to a project, perhaps "forgetting" to include them in the meeting invitation or conducting client visits without them. The ostracized employees then lack the information and interpersonal contacts they need to effectively do their work. Alternatively, an abrasive leader might isolate an employee by gradually taking away his or her responsibilities, delegating and reassigning them until the employee has little work of any importance to do. This can have dramatic effects on self-esteem and can make the employee vulnerable to layoffs.

Abrasive leaders are also known to use discrimination to undermine employees they feel threatened by. An abrasive boss might batter an employee with nearly constant criticism of her work, then throw her further off balance with overly personal remarks and uncomfortable compliments. For example, if an older, male boss sees a young, attractive trainee at her desk, deep in concentration on her work, he might set her off balance by greeting her with, "Hey, sexy, you look hot today—do you have a date tonight?"

Even if one sets aside the extremely inappropriate name-calling, such a comment is discriminatory and offensive. The young woman is striving to establish herself in the workplace and build a professional reputation for herself, yet her boss's sexist comments belittle her and make her seem less competent, both to herself and to anyone else in earshot. When I have confronted coaching clients about similar comments, they deny any intention to harm, and they claim they were making a joke. Even if this is true, such behavior demonstrates a lack of social grace and emotional intelligence.

When they believe an employee is a threat, brilliant but abrasive jerks often try to isolate, undermine, or belittle that person to remove the threat.

Abrasive jerks can set employees apart from the pack not just through exclusion and discrimination, but through favoritism as well. Such treatment may seem more benign, but it has insidious effects that can spread throughout an organization. Abrasive bosses tend to have a black-and-white way of viewing the world. Employees are categorized as either brilliant or totally incompetent, and their work can be considered either terrific or worthless.

In our case study, Peter favors people who he thinks can get him the results he wants or who are unconditionally loyal to him. People who are consistently loyal to Peter do not trigger his instinctive threat responses, so, instead of seeing them as competition, he comes to view them as vehicles to help him reach his objectives. Other employees soon notice this favoritism and begin to wonder why the woman in the next cubicle is being heaped with praise and given all the plum projects, while they get nothing but unfair criticism and impossible deadlines. The imbalance breeds jealousy and resentment. Eventually, it breaks down healthy social alliances and working relationships. Employees who once collaborated well together now gossip behind each other's backs, projects suffer, and the whole organization feels the impact.

Abrasive Leadership's Costs to the Organization

- Absenteeism
- Stress-related illnesses and other negative health effects
- Employee turnover
- Talent attrition
- Cost of replacement hiring
- Absence of potential successors
- Lost productivity
- Lack of creativity
- Cost of litigation for harassment, a hostile work environment, or discrimination
- Damage to the organization's reputation as a result of legal action and bad press
- Risk of retaliation, sabotage, and workplace violence
- Upper management's acceptance of an abrasive leadership style as the norm
- Low company-wide morale
- Reduced customer satisfaction
- Difficulty of developing a successor for the abrasive leader, given that such leaders do not foster competition

WORKPLACE AGGRESSION'S NEGATIVE EFFECTS ON INDIVIDUALS

Let's return to our case study to explore the specific effects Peter's toxic behavior has had on this particular organization. After their conversation with Lauren, the group had a new understanding of what motivates abrasive leaders' aggressive actions. Now, they were interested in looking at the impact Peter's behavior had been having on their company. Were the effects isolated to just the people he targeted, or did they spread across his division or even the company as a whole?

Tom opened the discussion, saying, "I would like to know what Peter's behavior costs the company, besides the high turnover that we've seen in his division."

Frank put in, "People seem to get sick more often in his division than in others."

"Yes," said Tom, "so more absenteeism. Peter's perturbing behavior has cost the company 10 percent more in absenteeism during the last nine months. That's a pretty big increase. What else?"

"What I have noticed," answered Frank, "is that when Peter overcontrols his direct reports, they retaliate with passive resistance. When Peter asks three times a day for a report he requested and hovers over their shoulder, his direct reports start working recklessly just to get the job done quickly and avoid the stress of having Peter micromanaging them. Other people who have dealt with his explosive temperament or his condescension start to quietly sabotage his projects."

"Here you see coworkers reacting to the leader's behavior instead of doing what is best for the company," Lauren commented. "When this happens, the result is lower productivity and risk of retaliation, sabotage, and even workplace violence."

"Well said," put in George. "People worry more about not provoking the boss than they care about getting good results. They're just interested in devising strategies to keep the boss from coming down on them. As Tom said, absenteeism has increased dramatically in Peter's division. My guess is that employees are calling in sick because of the stress caused by his behavior. Health costs are increasing, too, so it's likely that the stress of dealing with Peter is actually affecting employees' health."

* * *

George is quite likely correct in his assumption. An extensive body of research shows that, in addition to the damage stress does to mental health, it has a whole host of negative effects on physical health as well.[2] Stress is essentially a survival response, triggering the fight-or-flight instinct discussed in Chapter 3. When under stress, the human body shows increased levels of cortisol; if the stress becomes chronic, the raised cortisol levels can damage cardiovascular health, immune response, metabolism, and the autonomic nervous system.

To deal with stress, people tend to turn to coping behaviors that have their own negative impact on health: smoking, unhealthy diet, increased alcohol consumption, and poor sleep, for example.[3] They neglect their own health needs in an effort to narrow their focus and just get themselves through the stressful time. The end result is that employees tend to get sick more often, because their immune response is lowered, and are more likely to develop chronic health conditions. These problems cost them time away from work and raise the organization's employee health insurance expenditures.

The negative consequences of workplace bullying go beyond the bullied individual, however. Frequently, they spread to other people in the organization, too. When Hansen and colleagues explored the health outcomes of bullying at work, they discovered, in addition to the predictable depression and anxiety, that people who had been bullied at work received *less social support* from their coworkers and supervisors.[4] In other words, as the bullying persisted, the victims' colleagues and even their supervisor backed away, withdrawing support.

What's more, the researchers found that people who witnessed bullying showed increased anxiety, as well. Clearly, workplace bullying cannot be excused or ignored. Its impact has a ripple effect that spreads gradually outward and can eventually contaminate the entire organization.

WORKPLACE AGGRESSION'S NEGATIVE EFFECTS ON TEAMS

In John's office, the conversation about workplace aggression continued. Frank observed, "Peter also feels discomfort when he lacks control during brainstorming sessions. Brainstorming is a divergent process that builds on several people's ideas. Instead of letting the creative process flow naturally, Peter needs to control it. He starts interrupting and requesting details. Peter is so uncomfortable with a free-flowing approach and has such a desire to control that he forces participants to converge to a well-formulated decision before the idea has even gotten off the ground. Of course, he criticizes brainstorming sessions as sloppy thinking."

"Peter is a perfectionist," replied Lauren, "and the consequence is that many budding ideas are squashed before they have a chance to flourish into a service or product. On the one hand, Peter's sharp intellect, which is quick to root out faulty logic, can stimulate better thinking. On the other hand, if he interrupts the creative process repeatedly, his team members won't dare to speak up or volunteer ideas. The effect on the team's productivity can be substantial."

"Employees have also come to realize that Peter is not above stealing other people's ideas and presenting them as his own," George commented, "which doesn't encourage active participation or information sharing. People have learned to guard their ideas more closely to ensure that they get the credit they deserve for their work."

"Recognition is a strong motivator," said Lauren. "Besides, if organizations don't clearly reprimand such theft of ideas, coworkers come to believe it is an effective means to get ahead and begin to emulate the behavior. The toxic practice spreads like a virus, and creativity is lost."

In an aggressive organizational culture, employees are hesitant to share ideas. Workplace creativity is significantly decreased.

"Another source of creativity is cross-fertilization between divisions," said Frank. "This isn't happening. Turf protection discourages information sharing and collaboration. Peter's tendency to dominate the conversation, combined with his inability to listen, keeps him from effectively using team members' resources and ideas. Because people aren't likely to voice their ideas in this situation, Peter is apt to get even more frustrated and become more authoritarian in an attempt to force them to speak up. You can imagine what effect that has on the creative process. So, on a company level, productivity decreases. On an individual level, motivation and morale decrease. And on a team level, fewer ideas are shared."

WORKPLACE AGGRESSION'S NEGATIVE EFFECTS ON THE ORGANIZATION

"Peter is outstandingly intelligent and wants results," Lauren stated. "If he weren't so brilliant, he might not have been so successful up until now. There is a solution to this that we shall discuss later. For now, I'm wondering what other costs to the organization you have observed."

"Well, we have lost some customers—but revenues have increased in his division. I don't understand that," noted Gabrielle.

"Expand on that. What's the link between lost customers and abrasive leaders?"

Gabrielle answered, "If a lack of collaboration exists within the organization and a culture of disservice is prevalent, customers will pick up on this and simply go elsewhere. A lot of studies have shown that people prefer to buy from someone they have developed a rapport with."

Christopher added, "If you feel disrespected and demotivated by your leader, you just don't bother going the extra mile for your customers."

"It can destroy the company's reputation when demoralized and injured employees react abruptly to clients or when disillusioned employees leave the company and tell tales about how unhappy they were there," said Gabrielle. "Being served with lawsuits for discrimination or becoming known for abusive leadership certainly does nothing to enhance the company's reputation. As this negative reputation spreads, it becomes more difficult to attract talent."

*   *   *

The literature supports Gabrielle's assertion. Employees who are bullied are significantly more likely to leave a job than those who are not.[5] This turnover comes at a considerable cost to the organization, which must bear the expense of conducting a candidate search and training new hires. Turnover also imposes significant costs to productivity: Managers

are forced to devote work time to conducting interviews, and efficiency is reduced while new hires get up to speed in their position.

Yet the risk for such turnover is widespread across organizations. The Creative Center for Leadership found that 74 percent of successful executives in three Fortune 100 corporations have had at least one intolerable boss.[6] Given that a difficult relationship with a superior is one of the primary reasons people leave jobs, according to a Gallup poll, it would be wise for organizations to begin paying greater heed to the leadership style of their managers and intervening where necessary.[7]

*   *   *

"My concern about firing a person like this," contributed John, "is that a company can be put in jeopardy if the person has no clear successor. When employees in key positions leave, they create a void. In all fairness, Peter has had to turn around the division, and developing successors understandably has not been on his priority list. That being said, the lack of an appropriate replacement for Peter puts the company in a difficult situation today. I have asked him several times to start grooming his successor. Even if I were thinking of firing him, there is no one with sufficient leadership skill to replace him."

"A lack of a successor is another important cost," commented Lauren. "Without a likely replacement for Peter, you might feel as if your hands are tied. His toxic behavior is causing problems that are starting to spread beyond his own division, but you can't let him go because there's no one else to step in and carry on the work he has done to revitalize his division."

"In that case, we definitely don't want to fire him," said Jean. "He might not be perfect, but he's getting results, and we'll lose a lot of ground if we have to do a candidate search."

"There's one other important impact on the organization that no one has mentioned yet," noted Lauren. "An abrasive leader's bullying is like a virus; it spreads like wildfire through organizations. If it's not curtailed, it can be perceived as the acceptable or even desired corporate leadership style, and it becomes the norm. Therefore, it's in the organization's best interest to communicate its management and leadership principles, so that it's absolutely clear what leadership behaviors are encouraged and what abrasive behavior is unacceptable."

"Okay," said Frank. "That makes sense. But how do we do that?"

"That's a conversation we should devote some time to," said Lauren. "Why don't we break for lunch, and we can talk about it this afternoon when we're fresh?"

Chapter Review Questions

1. What are some of the costs of an abrasive leader's behavior on the individual, teams, and the organization?
2. What are the advantages of Peter's behavior that allowed him to turn around the struggling Asia division?
3. What are some of the intangible costs to the organization if an abrasive leader's behavior persists?

CHAPTER 5

TREATING THE VIRUS

How Organizations Can Encourage Healthy Behavior at the Organization, Team, and Individual Levels

---

After lunch, everyone ambled back into John Barbey's office. George was already seated at the conference table and was fidgeting with his pen, visibly anxious to get the meeting started again. After the coffee tray had been brought in and people began filling their cups, John made a start.

"Lauren and I had lunch together," he said, "and we talked a little further about her suggestion that the company needs to put a code of conduct into place to clearly communicate what behaviors we expect from our employees and what we consider unacceptable. We also discussed some actions the company can take to create a new culture of empowerment and accountability. That should help to diagnose abrasive leadership and encourage better leadership practices among our managers."

"One of the most important ways to create this culture of accountability is through the organization's values statement and the management principles," said Lauren. "These should be placed prominently everywhere possible, to keep them highly visible and to indicate the importance the company places on them. And they should be referred to in workshops, evaluations, and conferences, so they truly become part of the corporate culture."

FOSTERING A HEALTHY CORPORATE CULTURE AT THE ORGANIZATIONAL LEVEL

One of the reasons a strong, healthy corporate culture is so important is that behaviors are the outcome of a mind-set. If a leader's mind-set is that his or her employees are inherently lazy and need to be flogged into action, that's how he or she will treat them. That attitude will spread down the chain, poisoning the corporate culture. Therefore, changes in behavior cannot be accomplished without changes in mind-set. To illustrate this point to the group in the meeting room, Lauren drew their attention to a key section of Tempus's management principles.

"'Living up to Tempus's management principles is a commitment and a responsibility for everyone in our company,'" she read. "'To be effective, engaging and inspiring, all Tempus employees must "walk the talk" and lead by example in their daily work; in this context, actions speak louder than words.'"

"Our management principles are good. But how can we ensure that employees at all levels truly understand them?" asked Frank.

"Management needs to keep the principles in mind and reference them every day. Otherwise, the company's values and leadership principles are just talk, and we risk creating cynics," said Lauren.

"Are these management principles integrated into leaders' speeches?" she asked. "Are they discussed at kick-off meetings when a new project is launched? Are tasks and results the only topic of conversation in meetings, or do team leaders also address how and in what way tasks are to be accomplished?"

Ways to Make the Code of Conduct and Management Principles Part of Corporate Culture

- Communicate to all employees, including supervisors, managers, and executives, that the organization will not tolerate bullying to any degree. The code of conduct should explicitly state that employees who violate this principle will be disciplined and may be terminated.
- Clearly define bullying and indicate the specific behaviors that are considered unacceptable. The Society for Human Resources Management has provided an excellent template for organizations to use.[1]
- Post the code of conduct and management principles prominently in meeting rooms, break rooms, and other common areas.
- Make them easy to locate on the company's website.
- Acquaint new employees with them during the onboarding and immersion process.

- Discuss them in workshops, at conferences, and at kickoff meetings for new projects.
- Integrate them into leaders' speeches.
- Make sure suppliers and coaches receive a copy.
- Have employees evaluate managers' leadership in annual or semiannual reviews.

ENCOURAGING HEALTHY BEHAVIOR AT THE INDIVIDUAL LEVEL

"Abrasive behavior can sometimes be mistaken for demanding behavior," Lauren said, "and people tend to excuse it… at least initially, until it becomes a crisis. Let's look at the ways we've excused Peter's destructive behavior instead of taking the opportunity to address it before it took deeper root.

"In our initial conversation this morning, one of you excused Peter because of his inexperience as a leader and said that the problem would resolve itself with time. Others thought the financial success Peter has brought to a failing division was reason enough to tolerate his abrasive behavior. This presumes that the profits Peter brings in outweigh any damage he might do in the course of achieving them. I think we've seen in our conversation this morning that this is not the case."

Organizations often overlook abrasive behavior or mislabel it as demanding leadership. This sends employees the message that such behavior is acceptable.

Several people nodded in agreement, and even Jean—who had spoken up so strongly in defense of Peter that morning—seemed to be almost convinced.

"As we talked about the reasons for Peter's behavior," Lauren continued, "someone also pointed out that he's going through a divorce. This would have an emotional impact on anyone, but it wouldn't necessarily provoke repeated abrasive behavior.

"Some of you saw the toxicity as a temporary problem. Turning around a division can be stressful. Aren't we all subject to abrasive behavior in moments of stress? Yes, at times, any of us might be abrasive, but, again, it's the repetitive nature of the destructive behavior that has a detrimental effect on those who are confronted with it."

George, visibly shaken, interrupted Lauren. "I think we should fire him."

Gabrielle objected, "Everyone agrees that Peter is brilliant and succeeds where others have failed. Firing him would be losing a valuable resource."

"There's no one to replace him right now or in the near future, anyway," John put in. "Either he hasn't wanted to groom a successor, or he hasn't had the time."

George was not convinced. "If Peter doesn't change his attitude, it will be him or me," he said. "I can't take his constant jabs anymore."

"John, you should talk to him," said Gabrielle. "Tell him his behavior is unacceptable according to the company's values. Explain that we have a collegial style, a polite Swiss way of interacting, and his abrupt approach clashes with our corporate culture."

All too often, companies are overly results oriented. Leaders tend to be preoccupied with *what* needs to be done and what key performance indicators to monitor, but they rarely pay attention to *how* the work is to be done and whether employees are using acceptable behaviors to achieve those good results. This focus on outcome over methods allows toxic behavior to remain unchecked for years.

Performance Evaluations That Encourage Healthy Behavior

- Templates for employees' annual performance evaluations should clearly emphasize the task, desired outcomes, and key performance indicators for each individual.

- Evaluation templates should include space for the manager to indicate how goals and objectives were reached.
- Performance reviews should consider not just the employee's accomplishments but also the quality of his or her interactions with colleagues.
- Employees should have an opportunity to evaluate their manager's leadership qualities.
- Performance evaluations should be linked to the management principles (e.g., 60 percent of the annual performance evaluation for managers could focus on the leader's task at hand, and 40 percent could be benchmarked against the management principles).

"I agree that he has to change," said John. "We can't afford to have any more people leave his division. But what happens if he takes it badly? His work is everything to him. He might react emotionally and quit right then and there, and we can't afford to lose him."

Lauren interrupted, "It's likely that his family interacted abrasively with each other or that this was typical behavior in some prior environment, so he believes it's appropriate and will become very defensive if told otherwise. He might also be in denial and unaware that he causes distress because he wants so badly to succeed.

"Furthermore, it is no use talking to Peter about being nicer with others, because interpersonal relationships are his blind spot, although he's so visionary in other areas. He has high IQ but little to no EQ. Discussing with Peter how he has bruised his relationship with a coworker is like talking about an elephant to a blind person. He might even excuse his own behavior and accuse the hurt employee of being incompetent or oversensitive."

George commented, "The problem is, Peter thinks his authoritarian leadership style is partly responsible for the success he's had. Why can't he see that his strength is his outstanding strategic ability and that he's sabotaging himself with his lack of interpersonal skills?"

SUPPORTING HEALTHY INTERPERSONAL BEHAVIOR ON TEAMS

"He does have an inner circle of some of the brightest employees who follow him," added Frank, "but whether they can sustain the pace over the long term without burning out is another question. They're already working more than sixty hours a week *and* on weekends. Peter's division will be put in jeopardy if he loses any more of his resources. It takes us approximately two years to bring new recruits up to speed with the expertise they need to do their work effectively."

Fostering Healthy Interactions at the Team Level

- Create a team chart at the kickoff to new projects, to identify how team members will work together and interact. Be very specific as to what behaviors are and are not desired. All team members should agree to the team chart and sign it as a symbol of their commitment.
- When a new project team is formed, conduct a team coworker

assessment (e.g., Belbin Team Inventory, Prédom[i]) to get better acquainted with each team member's expertise and preferred role on the team.

- Make sure everyone on the team knows why they were selected and what is expected from them.
- Refer to the company's leadership principles or code of ethics before a project, and make sure the team chart is aligned with the principles.

"We could send him to a workshop on how to develop people skills," suggested Jean.

George countered, "He'll think that's just 'warm, fuzzy HR stuff' and not what true leaders do. And even if he recognized the need to improve his interpersonal skills, he wouldn't know what to do about it."

"You're right about that," said Gabrielle. "Just because Peter might be aware that he has hurt people's feelings doesn't mean he knows how to change his way of interacting."

Frank asked, "What do you think about offering him coaching, Lauren? With some experienced executive coach, I mean, who knows how to deal with this kind of problem."

Lauren thought about the question. "Before coming to Tempus, I worked for MKB Excellent Executive Coaching as a professional coach. MKB Excellent Executive Coaching is a boutique firm in Geneva that specializes in coaching abrasive leaders and global leaders in transition, and we had significantly positive results. We helped clients who were at the point of being fired before coaching completely turn their leadership style around. One of these clients, a talented and ambitious young woman, was eventually nominated by her direct reports as a candidate for exemplary leader of the year."

---

i   The Prédom provides a snapshot of individuals' behavioral strategies and actions. It explains why respondents are comfortable in some situations and not in others, as well as why they can easily communicate with some people but have difficulty with others.

Critical Actions to Create a
Culture of Empowerment and Accountability

- Organizations need to establish their management and leadership principles as a reference for desired behavior.
- Leaders should be evaluated on how they are performing (being) as leaders, not only on what results they are achieving (doing). Emphasis must be placed not only on *what* they achieve but on *how* they achieve it.
- Misconduct should be identified and communicated to the leader as quickly as possible.
- If they are receptive, abrasive leaders should be offered the support of a customized coaching program to help them change their destructive behaviors and leverage their strengths.
- Organization heads should communicate to their abrasive leaders that they are valued but that misbehavior has consequences, which will be applied.

As she finished speaking, Lauren's mobile phone began to vibrate. She looked down at the screen, then glanced at Frank, who sat next to her, and showed him the text she had just received. Frank explained to the team that another incident had just occurred in Peter's division. Robert had resigned. He'd just walked out, without even giving advance notice. John let out a sigh, looked at Lauren, and nodded his head to indicate that it was okay for her to go find out exactly what had happened. They watched her leave, even more certain now that the time had come to take action.

"Now we're definitely in a crisis situation," John said grimly. "Let's hire a coach immediately. Frank, do you have a firm in mind?"

Frank said, "I'd suggest MKB Excellent Executive Coaching, since they specialize in coaching brilliant and abrasive leaders. Unfortunately, they're opening new offices in the United States and likely wouldn't be able to kick-start the coaching process in Switzerland for another month. But since Lauren is so knowledgeable, what about asking her to coach Peter?"

John was disinclined to go this route and preferred to have Lauren serve as an impartial observer to advise him in this situation. He thought Peter might resist opening up to Lauren because they interacted so often professionally.

"We need someone else," he stated firmly. "Amanda, in our HR department, has coaching experience. Let's call her in and have her meet Peter to determine whether they can begin coaching work together. I want to get this process moving as quickly as possible before any more damage is done."

Just then, John's assistant put her head around the door to remind him of his next appointment.

"Okay, thank you, Frank, for organizing this meeting," said John. "Keep us posted. I'm looking forward to getting this problem solved and keeping good people on board!"

Chapter Review Questions

1. How do people often excuse toxic behavior in others?
2. When does abrasive behavior become detrimental to the organization?
3. Why is transferring a brilliant and abrasive leader like Peter to another division not an effective solution?
4. What critical actions should organizations implement to create a culture of empowerment and accountability?
5. What measures foster healthy interactions at the team level?

CHAPTER 6

AMANDA'S MEETING WITH PETER

Common Reasons Why Coaching Fails

As soon as the meeting broke up for the day, George contacted Amanda and asked her to come in for a meeting. He hadn't discussed this with Lauren, but he was eager to get the problem solved now that the group had decided on an approach. Dealing with Peter's outbursts had been taking a toll on George, and he felt worn down and close to burnout.

When George had briefed Amanda on the situation as it stood, they agreed that she would meet with Peter for an introductory session. She

55

was surprised to be selected for such a challenging task, given that she was not Peter's peer; she thought Frank should be the one to work with Peter on the problem, but did not voice her concerns. Because she had just finished her coaching training, she was very eager to meet the challenge. She wanted to seem confident and capable, so she did not ask any further questions about the situation before she approached Peter.

Rather than contacting Peter's assistant to arrange a meeting, Amanda decided to just stop by Peter's office right away. She hoped this more casual approach would take some of the pressure off of their conversation. Amanda was nervous about the meeting with Peter and paused to take a few deep breaths before she tapped on his office door. She hadn't met Peter personally before, but she knew enough of his reputation to be worried about how he might react to what she had to say.

"Hello, come in," called a deep voice from inside the room.

Amanda stepped into the office. The room was almost empty. She saw an impressive desk, two chairs, and Peter's many sporting and professional trophies on the only shelf in the room. A few papers were neatly organized on his desk. "Might he be a perfectionist?" was Amanda's first thought.

There was a large window on the far wall, and in the bright sunlight streaming in, it was difficult to make out Peter's face. But as she approached the desk, she saw that he was a tall, handsome man with jet-black hair and green eyes. The fact that he was so attractive and physically emanated power made him all the more intimidating.

"Hello, Peter," she said, wishing she sounded more confident. "I'm Amanda, from HR. I am not sure you are aware, but the company offers all its executives the opportunity to work with a coach if they wish . . ."

Brilliant but abrasive jerks often react aggressively when they feel cornered or ambushed, so avoid putting them on the defensive.

Peter seemed annoyed by her presence, so Amanda decided that getting straight to the point might be the best approach. "I wondered if you might be interested. I can coach you if you like."

Peter was immediately on the defensive. "Was this Frank's idea? Did he send you here?" he demanded in a husky voice. He approached her, looking intently first into her eyes and then slowly down her body. "I don't want to be coached, and I don't have the time!" he snapped.

"Well, a surprising number of people have left your division recently. How can you explain that?" asked Amanda, fidgeting with the papers she was holding. She felt awkward just standing there in the middle of the room, but Peter had not asked her to sit down.

"So Frank sent you, huh? If only HR did what they were supposed to do and hired competent people!" he accused. With an irritated sigh, he looked away from Amanda and turned his attention back to his computer screen. She had managed to annoy him in just a few minutes of conversation.

"Okay," said Amanda. "Can your division handle its workload with such a reduced staff?" She was not going to be dismissed so easily.

"Look, I'd rather have a few good people around than a lot of dead wood. Why are you in my office?" He seemed irritated that she was still in the room.

"So, is the work being performed well?" Amanda persisted. "Are you achieving your objectives?"

"Yes, my work is being performed perfectly," Peter declared. "I managed to turn around this division when everyone else failed," he said, amused that she was trying so hard to assert herself.

"Have you attained your objectives?" Amanda asked.

"Is this an interrogation or what? You HR people should do what you're paid for! Find me some competent people instead of snooping in everyone's office and wasting our time!"

"It sounds like you have an issue with HR," Amanda observed. "How much time do you typically take to deal with issues affecting your staff? What are you doing to solve the turnover problem in your division?"

SUPPORT, NOT BETRAYAL

"Look," said Peter, enjoying watching Amanda floundering and desperate to get his attention. "I bring in 60 percent of the revenue for the Asia division, and I'm tired of holding the whole department up almost single-handedly." Peter paused, and his attitude seemed to shift. "I need HR to do its job so I can do mine, Amanda," he said softly, curious to see how she would respond.

"So what if you did your own hiring?" Amanda wondered. "What would your staff look like?"

"Well, that would be difficult. I'm already bringing in 60 percent of the revenue for this division." He was getting angry again. "I am not paid to hire people! You are!"

"What is this situation costing you?" asked Amanda, red in the face.

"What situation? I work all the time, weekends included. I need more competent people. I need to meet my deadlines. You need to do your job instead of asking me stupid questions," he snapped, noticing how pretty she looked when she was flustered.

"What if I told you that I could help you improve your productivity by 30 percent, and it wouldn't cost you a dime? Would you try it?" asked Amanda, grasping at anything that might get him to take this conversation more seriously.

"I would think you were crazy! What do you know about business development?" Peter thought for a moment. "Ideas can come from anywhere, and my top priority is results, so I guess I would listen to you, even though I'd have little hope that you could tell me anything new."

Many brilliant and abrasive leaders are logical and data-driven, so present them with hard facts and statistics whenever possible.

"Are you willing to try?" Amanda asked pleadingly.

"I don't know. Try what?"

"There's a pretty large body of research that shows that you can improve your productivity by 30 percent if you are more aware of the impact you have on others and if you can motivate them so that they obtain better results," said Amanda, aware that Peter was looking at her more intently now.

"Believe me," answered Peter, still amused by this young, pretty woman's courage, "I motivate them every day. I am motivating them all the time. The ones who didn't move fast enough have left. I had too much dead wood on my team. I was in the U.S. Air Force for many years, and I can tell you—those guys who left wouldn't have lasted an afternoon in boot camp. They can't take the pressure. I need people who are proactive."

"Ah, proactive. They aren't proactive?" Amanda asked, latching on to one of Peter's employment criteria.

"No, they aren't. They don't move. In my team of seven direct reports, three are okay. At least they aren't stupid, lethargic, and incompetent."

"Tell me about your relationship with your boss."

Peter stiffened, and his face closed off. "What about it?" he asked belligerently. "My boss, John, used to lead this division, and he did really well. Then two directors followed between John and me. They drove this division into the ground. I'm performing better than George did in this role, and we've been bringing in more profits since I restructured the division. I need more competent people," he reasserted. "Do you understand?"

Common Coaching Mistakes

- *Communicating for management:* Let management communicate with the client about what behaviors will not be tolerated. Coaches should not be the messengers; leaders must take responsibility.
- *Engaging in fact battles:* As the coach, you have not witnessed the abrasive behavior. Therefore, don't debate the facts. Keep a neutral stance, and hear both sides.
- *Showing bias:* Don't be influenced only by the victims of the brilliant and abrasive jerk. Consider the data from all stakeholders equally, including the client.
- *Being overprotective:* Don't let a desire to protect either your client or the organization put you in the middle.
- *Tolerating bad behavior:* Encourage the client to behave better and the company to make organizational changes to stop workplace bullying.
- *Being intimidated:* When you're intimidated or worried about being competent enough to coach an abrasive jerk, your attention is on you. Refocus on listening to the client and key stakeholders.
- *Ignoring the organization's system:* If the brilliant and abrasive

jerk tries to engage more productively with coworkers, they may misinterpret the behavior as being manipulative. Stakeholders need to know that the client is undergoing a coaching leadership program to address his or her abrasive behaviors. This way, even if the attempts to change are awkward, stakeholders will know the leader is trying to improve rather than being manipulative.

"I am confused," Amanda broke in. Her anxiety about failing this interaction was beginning to cloud her thinking. "When you refer to 'your boss,' are you talking about your current boss, George, or the CEO, John Barbey?"

"John Barbey, of course. George is just an administrative person. He has brought in little to no business. He adds no value to the company whatsoever."

Amanda shifted gears again, but her voice weakened. "What would you do if you had more people?"

"I would have better results if you did your job correctly."

"What does George think about your performance?" Amanda countered.

"I don't know. Ask him! Didn't he send you here? He's too apprehensive to speak to me directly."

Gathering up all her courage, Amanda asked, "Tell me about outperforming him. Is that important to you?"

"Well, yes, I think that's important," Peter replied. "John Barbey is the CEO. He's a tough act to follow." Peter's tone mellowed when he talked about John. It was clear how much he admired the man. Amanda noticed that Peter kept referring to John as his boss.

"John? In what way?"

"He was given a lot more people than I have," Peter said. "He did really well. It's harder now because the economy is lagging."

"How do you behave?" asked Amanda. "How do you communicate with your direct reports?"

"I meet with them once a week."

"That's not *how*," said Amanda. "Tell me *how* you communicate with them."

He was no longer listening to her. "Did John send you here today?" he broke in.

Amanda hesitated but thought it best to say yes. He might take her more seriously if he knew that John had asked her to coach him.

Peter looked dismayed to hear this and answered Amanda's question defensively. "I meet with them once a week, and I give them the week's results. We review them and strategize about what can be improved. This gives us a few leads to go after. I ask them how they intend to tackle the market and meet their objectives. I tell them what to do after asking them what ideas they have."

"Are you affirming?" Amanda asked. "Are you assertive when you talk to them? Are you considerate?" Amanda noticed Peter was no longer amused but seemed preoccupied with his thoughts.

"I'm professional. I get results."

"And are you actually getting results?" ventured Armanda, then immediately regretted her question.

"Don't you ever look at the quarterly results?" Peter snapped. "Are they too complicated for you? I told you, I bring in 60 percent of the division's revenues." Peter paused and sighed. "I need good people. It's getting hard to bring in revenue in this down market."

Amanda said, "I had a conversation with Frank, who basically told me that unless you improve your behavior, John is going to fire you. How do you feel about that?"

Peter became extremely agitated on hearing this news. "What the hell are you saying?" he exclaimed. "Who the hell are you? Look, they are crazy if they fire me! I bring in 60 percent of the division's revenue single-handedly! What did John say? So they're going to fire me, you say, and then what?"

"Do you want to get fired?" Amanda asked.

"What a stupid question!" Peter shouted. "Would you like to get fired?" Grabbing a paperweight off his desk, he threw it at the closet door.

Amanda was frightened now, but she summoned all her strength and, despite her trembling hands, managed to speak. She felt disembodied, as if she weren't really the one saying the words. "You said you're a professional. You seem to really like your job, even though it comes with a lot of stress."

Peter cut her off. "Look, I am firing *you*. I have a lot to do now and no time to waste on this crap! Get the hell out of here."

After Amanda had fled, nearly in tears, Peter stormed out of his own office and headed straight for John Barbey's. He blew past John's assistant and barged straight into John's office, demanding to know what was going on.

John managed to calm Peter down and reassured him that he was a valued member of the team. But he also warned Peter that if any more of his direct reports left or filed harassment or discrimination suits, John would be forced to fire him. John explained that the company was offering Peter a coach to support him in changing his interpersonal leadership style. Peter started raising his voice, but he managed to contain himself. He had enormous respect for John, who had, over the years, established himself as a well-regarded and extremely successful business tycoon who now owned a sizable portion of the city. Peter was hurt and insulted that John would send a low-level employee like Amanda to talk to him, instead of coming to meet with Peter in person.

Now Peter was depressed; he felt betrayed by John, whom he had looked up to as a father figure. He felt that the sacrifices he had made for the company, working night and day for so many months, had gone unappreciated. He had no desire to work with a coach but felt coerced, since he realized that John was giving him an ultimatum. He could not understand why John was turning against him, after he had made heroic efforts to turn the company around and achieved such impressive results. George must have been lobbying against him.

Peter's mood might have been entirely different if Amanda had handled their initial meeting differently. If she had been better informed about the situation and approached him with more tact and EQ, Peter might have seen the offer of coaching as an opportunity to increase his performance and get even better results. In the following chapter, we'll explore what Amanda could have done differently, and how to apply those lessons to your own organization or coaching practice.

Chapter Review Questions

1. What mistakes did Amanda make when coaching Peter?
2. What strength did she demonstrate?
3. What could Amanda have done differently to get a better response from Peter?

CHAPTER 7

LAUREN'S MENTORING

The Excellent Executive Coaching Process

After her disastrous conversation with Peter, Amanda was mortified and struggling not to cry. Since this was her very first coaching assignment, she had wanted so badly to do a good job and prove herself. Instead, she'd just made the situation even worse. She couldn't understand what she had done wrong.

Amanda knew she wouldn't be able to get any work done when the debacle with Peter was weighing so heavily on her mind, so she went straight to Lauren's office in hope of gaining some insight into what had gone wrong. She burst in without knocking and found the HR manager sitting at her computer, deep in concentration. Amanda blurted out, "Well, that was a disaster. Peter obviously doesn't want to work with me. I have no idea what went wrong."

Lauren tried to calm Amanda down. "Hold on, Amanda," she said. "Stop shaking. Tell me about your conversation with Peter."

"I would be grateful for your feedback," pleaded the disheartened Amanda. "I'd like to know what I should have done differently."

Lauren listened carefully as Amanda went over the key points of her conversation with Peter, then asked, "First of all, Amanda, what was the objective for your first meeting with Peter?"

"To engage him in a coaching process," Amanda replied, as if that should have been evident.

"Okay, that's *your* objective, not his," answered Lauren. "What information did you gather before you went into Peter's office? I wish I could have briefed you before you talked with him."

Company executives need to fulfill their leadership role and set clear boundaries for their direct reports. Other employees and the coach should take care not to interfere with the responsibilities of management and serve as the bearer of bad news. This tactic can backfire.

"Well, George told me I had to convince Peter to agree to be coached because he has such problems with interpersonal relationships and because six people have left his division in the last year."

Lauren asked, "Did you find out what George has already done to address the problem? What has he done about Peter's lack of interpersonal skills? Has George talked to him about the consequences if he does not change?"

Lauren also wanted to know whether the company had tried any other kind of intervention to address Peter's abrasiveness. For instance, Peter could have been invited to attend a workshop on interpersonal relations. Also, John, as head of the company and someone Peter greatly admired, could have met with Peter directly to discuss his concerns about the multiple losses of human capital in the division.

"Did you find out whether John, George, or Frank had fulfilled their management role by explaining to Peter that they wanted to see a change in his interpersonal behavior?"

In response to Lauren's questions, Amanda said, "I guess I was influenced by Peter's bad press and thought to protect him by informing him of the consequences he might face. I also wanted to justify my reasons for coming to see him."

"Right. What model or process were you working with when you talked to him?" asked Lauren. "It might be helpful keep that in mind as we review the conversation."

"Model or process?" Amanda was confused. "I'm not sure what you mean."

Lauren walked up to the whiteboard that hung in her office and started drawing. She said, "Let me walk you through a good coaching process, and then we can review the conversation you had with Peter."

The Excellent Executive Coaching Process

In my executive coaching work, I have developed an effective approach for working with brilliant but abrasive jerks: the Excellent Executive Coaching Process. This process is designed to help clients close the gap between their reality and their goal or desired outcome. The overall structure keeps the conversation useful and focused. In addition, the Excellent Executive Coaching Process offers a more predictable progress toward the client's goals than some other models afford.

The Excellent Executive Coaching Process is not based on giving advice or telling clients what to do. Instead, it's a Socratic questioning approach that guides clients toward their *own* solutions. The coach's role is to help clients move from a state of denial to awareness by providing very specific feedback about their abrasive words and actions.[1] The key components of behavior change for brilliant jerks are insight and self-awareness.

The Excellent Executive Coaching Process is grounded in the International Coach Federation's core competencies, which focus on setting a strong foundation for coaching, building a mutually trusting relationship with the client, communicating well, and guiding the client through learning and change.[2]

Laying the Foundation for the Coaching Process

The first step in the Excellent Executive Coaching Process is building rapport—that is, establishing trust with the client, employee, or leader by creating a safe, supportive environment that fosters ongoing, mutual respect. The very first coaching session starts the process of building rapport by letting the coach and client decide whether they want to work together; this is often called a "chemistry meeting."

The process of building rapport continues throughout coaching. For instance, if the brilliant jerk acts disrespectfully to the coach, the coach should use the interaction as a teaching moment to help the leader question his or her behavior. When Amanda approached Peter unexpectedly, without an appointment and without letting him know in advance what she wanted to discuss, she put him on the defensive and failed to establish clear agreement and trust.

Given Peter's reaction to Amanda, it would have been better to open by discussing the value he had added to the organization, rather than jumping straight to his failings. He likely wanted a chance to boast about his accomplishments. Amanda then could have responded by showing appreciation for his success. That would have created some positive energy between them—that is, built rapport—before she dove into the behaviors Peter needed to change.

* * *

Lauren explained the Excellent Executive Coaching Process to Amanda in detail, beginning with the first step, building rapport. "Rapport is essential before any significant coaching work is possible," she told Amanda. "The first meeting with a client is often referred to as a 'chemistry test' or an exploratory meeting. It helps to determine whether you can work together."

Step 1 of the Excellent Executive Coaching Process: Build rapport with the client.

"Lauren, in your experience, have you always been able to create rapport?" Amanda wondered.

"I pride myself on being able to work with people of many different profiles and adapt to their styles. However, on one occasion, I was the spitting image of my client's wife. They happened to be going through a nasty divorce. After the initial chemistry meeting, I decided not to continue the coaching because I was concerned that my client would project his problems with his wife onto me, and I was convinced that another coach would better serve him."

Amanda nodded; that made sense.

"On another occasion," Lauren continued, "I had an exploratory meeting with a charming, bright lady who had a problem accepting compliments. After she talked with me for ten minutes, I asked whether I could take her hand. When she said yes, I held her hand gently and told her she was a wonderful person and very likable. How would you react in such a situation?"

Amanda answered, "I would feel really good about myself and might even give you a hug in return."

"Well, she pulled her hand away like it was on fire. When she realized how abruptly she had reacted, she blushed and apologized profusely. She then admitted she had been abused as a child and always felt dirty as a result. After empathizing with her pain, I told her that I was not the best person to help her, but that I could refer her to an excellent psychologist. I told her I would welcome her back into a coaching process after she had resolved this issue with a psychologist. Honesty means doing the best thing for your client, knowing your professional limitations, and helping your client to get the best professional advice and help for his or her needs."

Lauren then brought the subject back to Peter. "If he had a clear understanding of why the coaching was taking place and what he had to gain from it," she asked, "would this have helped create rapport?"

Amanda admitted that it would have. She felt embarrassed that she had barreled into the process without taking all the necessary steps.

"What agreement did you establish?" Lauren asked. "Did he feel that you had his best interests in mind?"

"Honestly, no," Amanda said. "It was not clear to him why he was being offered coaching. I did not verify with management what they had communicated to Peter and how he perceived the situation."

Once the coach has built rapport with the client and gotten him or her to agree to a coaching process, the next step is to meet with management to find out what steps have already been taken. It's important to know whether the leader's bosses have talked with him or her about the need for change and whether any consequences for failure to change have been discussed. Does the leader know what's at stake?

Step 2 of the Excellent Executive Coaching Process: Meet with management to learn what has been communicated to the client about the need for change. Determine what the client has been told about the potential consequences and the desired outcomes of the coaching process.

The third step in the Excellent Executive Coaching Process is defining short-, medium-, and long-term objectives—for both the key stakeholders and the client. Short-term objectives are the desired outcomes for each particular coaching session. Medium-term objectives are the desired outcomes for the next three to twelve months, and long-term objectives are the personal and professional situation the client and other stakeholders would like to see within the next three to five years. They can also include the individual's desired legacy.

When the goals have been established, the coach reviews the current situation. At this point, it is important to identify what barriers are hindering the client from reaching his or her goals, as observed by the client and by the key stakeholders.

Step 3 of the Excellent Executive Coaching Process: Define the client's short-, medium-, and long-term objectives. Identify the key stakeholders' objectives for the coaching in a triad with the client, the client's boss and HR, and the coach.

In Peter's case, his stakeholders view his abrasive leadership style as a stumbling block. If Peter does not address this issue, he could be fired. Therefore, this is remedial coaching, and Peter is unlikely to view it as developmental. It will take more work than usual for the coach to give the process a positive connotation.

It is important to keep in mind, however, that the coaching model is not a linear process. Sometimes the client may define an objective that is not the true issue at hand but points to a deeper, underlying need or problem. In this case, the coach should start the process over from the beginning to work on the underlying issue. The only difference is that progress may be faster the second time through, since rapport has already been established.

The Path to Positive Change

The fourth step of the Excellent Executive Coaching Process is coaching from the current situation. This step is focused on the present moment and helping clients resolve immediate interpersonal problems, rather than working toward longer-term objectives. If clients are clear about their current problems but frustrated and uncertain about the outcome they're hoping for, then it's important to start here, where the client has some clarity.

Conversely, some clients already know what they want to achieve from the coaching process and have a clear vision of their desired outcome, but are unsure how to resolve their current issues. In this case, the coach's role is to help clients work toward new insights, thought patterns, and perspectives that will help them resolve their current issues. For these clients as well, coaching should begin with Step 4, the current situation. It's important to start the coaching process where the energy is. During this step, the coach does the research work of finding out how the client is perceived, as well as having the client fill out inventories.

Step 4 of the Excellent Executive Coaching Process:
Coach from the current situation, by helping
clients resolve their immediate challenges.

When coaching from the current situation, help clients achieve enough resolution to give them a sense of progress, and allow them to vent, but be careful not to let them drown in negative energy or get bogged down in operational issues. As soon as possible, shift the orientation toward the longer-term goals, and lead clients to clarity about their desired outcome and about more strategic issues. This is Step 5 of the coaching process.

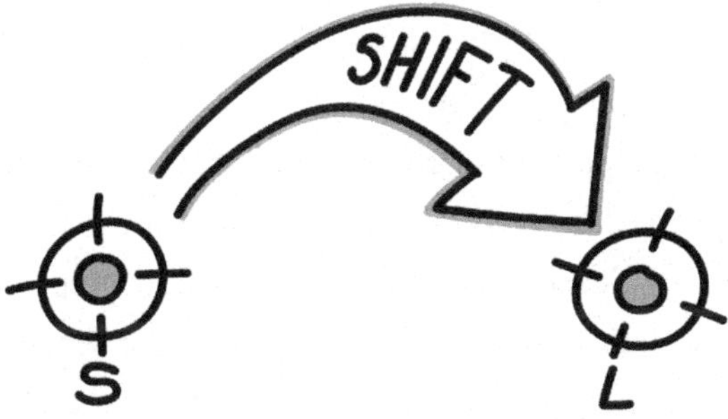

Although clients have already defined their long-term objectives in Step 3 of the process, Step 5 asks them to go deeper. Now, they are considering not just what they want to gain from the coaching process, but what they hope to achieve in the scope of their career and in their personal life. With the guidance of the coach, clients will explore how well their aspirations fit with the organization's strategy and mission, what they want to learn from their situation, and what shift needs to take place for them to succeed.

The case study offers a good illustration of this decision-making. Peter probably knows where he wants to lead his division, but he's unaware of or in denial about the realities of his current situation—that is, how destructive his leadership style is (Step 4). If the coaching started with Peter's current interpersonal abrasiveness, without feedback from the key stake-holders, the coach would be trying to help Peter resolve problems he is blind to and has no self-awareness about.

Step 5 of the Excellent Executive Coaching Process:
Create a clear long-term vision of the client's desired
personal and professional outcomes and how they may
align with the organization's strategy and mission.

For Peter, then, a good starting point would be to discuss where he wants to lead his division, which he will likely enjoy doing. Only then can the coaching begin to shed light on where he is blinded (his abrasiveness and the fact that he is perceived as a jerk).

Once the coach helps clients clarify what they aspire to (Step 5), the next step is to explore the gap between those aspirations and their current situation (Step 6). In Peter's case, the coach should help him understand what is holding him back from achieving his goal of eventually succeeding John as CEO. Only then will he be motivated to make changes, once he gains insight about what actions he needs to take.

Step 6 in the Excellent Executive Coaching Process:
Explore the gap between the client's current situation
and his or her desired outcome and aspirations.

Reviewing the Process

To encourage consistent progress toward the stated goals and objectives, at the end of each session the coach should review any new insights and ask the client his or her thoughts on the session. This is Step 7 of the

Excellent Executive Coaching Process. This review allows the coach to identify what shift in perspective the coaching session provided the client and help the coach customize the next step to further enhance the client's progress.

For example, the coach could ask, "What do you take away from this session?" This check-in not only provides the coach with information about what parts of the session were important for the client (which, in turn, will help the coach to customize the approach in future sessions), it also allows the client to review what useful nuggets of wisdom he or she learned from the coaching session and renew his or her commitment to implementing any changes that were discussed.

Step 7 of the Excellent Executive Coaching Process: Identify the client's insights and key takeaways from the session.

In Step 8, the client creates action plans to implement and decides on issues to think about or new behaviors to practice before the next session. The coach helps the client manage his or her progress and accountability. This step should happen after every session. Once Peter has gained enough insight— had an "aha moment"—the coach should help him create an action plan and encourage him while he implements it. Often, the stakeholders' feedback, once correctly debriefed with the client, can spark one of those moments.

Step 8 of the Excellent Executive Coaching Process: Help the client create and implement action plans.

After a series of coaching sessions, and only near the end of the coaching program, the coach briefly interviews the same key stakeholders again and writes up a short report to identify perceived progress made and next steps (Step 9 of the coaching process). The coach then debriefs this report with the client.

Step 9 of the Excellent Executive Coaching Process: Conduct brief interviews with stakeholders, and debrief with the client.

Finally, near the close of the coaching process, another triad meeting takes place among the boss, the client, and the coach to identify the progress the client has made and the next actions (Step 10). In some cases, HR personnel are included in this. Often, it depends on the HR personnel and the leader's place in the hierarchy.

Step 10 of the Excellent Executive Coaching Process: Conduct a final triad meeting among the client, the client's boss, and the coach.

PREPARING FOR THE FIRST MEETING WITH MANAGEMENT

In my years of executive coaching, I have found it is good practice to prepare for the first meeting with a client by asking the corporate sponsors why they decided on coaching as a means to address the issue. Find out whether they tried anything else before resorting to a coaching process. Did they send the employee to an interpersonal development workshop? Did the company implement a 360-Degree Feedback process to ask the client's boss, peers, and direct reports about his or her strengths and weaknesses?[i] Will the coaching be part of a workshop to help the participant implement in the work environment what he or she has learned? Has management already told the client what needs to improve?

In Peter's case, his superiors need to communicate their expectations of coaching and clearly spell out the consequences Peter will face if he doesn't change his behavior. If there is no pressure from management on Peter to change, why should he? His behavior has been extremely "successful" to date.

Amanda's initial attempt to work with Peter focused heavily on the consequences he might face if he failed to change. This information, I cannot repeat enough, *should be communicated by management*, not by the coach. Ideally, John or George should have spoken with Peter directly about the problems with his behavior and the actions the company would take if he did not improve. At that point, the coach should facilitate a conversation between Peter and management in a triad meeting to cover the following:

- establishing a coaching agreement that integrates the coaching agenda
- clearly indicating to stakeholders (mainly Peter's boss, George) that the coaching process is confidential
- identifying key performance indicators
- identifying the consequences Peter faces if he does not change his behavior, and the benefits if he does
- agreeing about what support Peter can expect from his boss and the CEO and how much time he has to show changes in his behavior
- assessing how willing Peter is to engage in a coaching process
- deciding exactly what is to be communicated in any reports on

---

i   The 360-Degree Feedback Report, which is popular among coaches and HR personnel, gives the coaching client anonymous feedback from his or her colleagues, including managers, peers, and direct reports.

the coaching process and when the next three-way meeting (i.e., client, management, and coach) will take place

- reinforcing that the coaching conversations are confidential.

This conversation among client, management, and coach ensures that everyone is on the same page. It also gives the coach a concrete record to refer to if the client is in denial or starts distorting reality to suit his or her ego during the coaching process.

Before entering into a coaching relationship, ensure that management have communicated clearly with the client about their expectations and the possible consequences. This information should never come from the coach.

In some cases, companies call in a coach but have already decided to fire the abrasive leader. They initiate a coaching process to show that they have tried everything before dismissing the employee. In these scenarios, a three-way conversation enables the client and his or her stakeholders to determine whether all parties are sincerely giving the client a second chance.[ii]

* * *

Amanda did not feel a three-way conversation with management was necessary, because she was just initiating an exploratory meeting,

---

ii   I insist on confidentiality, and any information I share with management is only shared during the three-way meetings. I state this in my coaching contracts. Why? Once, I was hired to coach an abrasive leader whom the company had already decided to fire. I was given six months to bring about tangible changes in the client's behavior. The coaching had barely begun when the employees staged a coup. They told top management that my client was to be fired, or all the employees would quit. Management asked me for a report of my interviews to use as support in firing the executive. If I didn't share the report, they wouldn't pay me. Of course, I refused, and I didn't get paid in full for my work. It is critical to know whether top management sincerely intends to give the client a second chance or simply considers coaching a step on the road to firing the executive.

also called a chemistry meeting. When she said this to Lauren, the older woman replied, "Often, the three-way conversation takes place after the initial exploratory meeting, but it's wise to ask what management has communicated to the client with regard to why he or she has been offered coaching."

"What else could I have done to be successful in my first meeting with Peter?" Amanda asked. "What comes after developing rapport and having a preparatory meeting with Peter and his bosses?"

"The next step is to get an overview of Peter's short-, medium-, and long-term goals," Lauren told her. "His short-term objectives are the goals he has for each separate coaching session. This includes a short-term desired outcome, which is clarified during the coaching sessions. What key performance indicators would inform both you and Peter that the coaching is on track and successful after your first meeting?"

Amanda thought about this for a moment. "It would be a successful meeting if Peter were willing to accept my coaching and were committed to engaging in the process."

"Absolutely!" agreed Lauren. "What do you think the key stakeholders' medium-term objectives are for Peter? What are Peter's objectives?"

"From what I understand," said Amanda, "Peter has a high IQ, but a low EQ. Coaching should help him to develop his interpersonal skills, including increasing his array of leadership styles, so that he can adapt to each person and situation with more leadership agility.

"For example, he would know when he needs to be the one to make a tough decision and when he should empower his direct reports instead.

He would understand when to be encouraging and when to be demanding. When he is frustrated, instead of having uncontrollable tantrums and attacking other people, he would be better at working out problems collaboratively."

"Right!" said Lauren. "What are Peter's medium-term objectives for himself?"

Amanda thought for a moment. "Increasing his results without burning out or harming his direct reports' confidence. Peter would work collaboratively with his peers and his boss, George. He would become more aware of his impact on others. He would be better at helping his direct reports increase their competencies, and he would be grooming a successor."

"No," Lauren disagreed, "these are not Peter's objectives. These are the key stakeholders' desired outcomes from the coaching."

Amanda realized that Lauren had a good point. She hadn't even been thinking about what Peter really wanted to achieve. "Yes, you are right," she said. "That's what Peter's boss and peers want him to get out of the coaching. I don't know what Peter wants. I didn't ask."

As a coach, make sure you are clear about
what the client's objectives are, not just
those of the key stakeholders.

Lauren asked, "How would Peter's key stakeholders know that he has changed? This will help you determine the key performance indicators or success criteria for coaching."

"Do you mean how would they know that coaching has had a positive effect on Peter? I guess his stakeholders would notice how Peter's behavior has changed. Fewer people would leave his division. He would cause fewer legal disputes. He would begin grooming a successor."

"Absolutely. As Peter's coach, Amanda, what would you look for as the key performance indicators?"

"Hmm. I'm not sure. Maybe the coach's objective would be that Peter gains insights that would transform the way he sees himself and others. He would understand how others see him and be able to adapt his behavior accordingly.

"He would need to be transformed in a profound enough way that he does not revert to his prior behavior, though. He would then be able to remain at the head of his division, have more career options, and, who knows, he could be the next CEO. He has the brains, but he needs the emotional intelligence to have stakeholders committed, engaged, and willing to follow him."

"In my experience," said Lauren, "sophisticated leaders adapt their leadership style to the situation and the person and are less prone to their internal fears—or, better said, they can manage their fears and anxiety in a more constructive way."

Amanda nodded in understanding. She could see now that she had jumped into her attempt to coach Peter much too abruptly, without taking the proper steps to ensure that all the stakeholders were on the same page. She should have approached Peter more diplomatically, taken the time to earn his trust and make sure she knew what he himself wanted to achieve from the coaching process, not just what management expected the outcome to be. She felt that she was learning a great deal from this conversation.

Step 3 of the Excellent Executive Coaching Process: Determining the Objectives of the Stakeholders and Client

Objectives	Key Stakeholders	Peter
Short-term	Peter will be less aggressive with his direct reports and colleagues. There will be fewer outbursts. His team will stabilize, as employee turnover slows.	Peter will understand why John wants him to receive coaching, despite his proven success.
Medium-term	Peter will exhibit stronger interpersonal skills, more flexibility in leadership style, and better control over his temper.	Peter will understand that the wind is not in his favor and, at this stage, want to understand why. (The coach's objective at this stage is that Peter will understand, through input from his key stakeholders, what is stopping him from progressing in his career.)
Long-term	Peter's behavior change will be evident, and his division will have fewer interpersonal problems. He will begin grooming a successor.	Peter will succeed John Barbey as CEO or be promoted to a similar role.

Lauren moved on to the final piece of the puzzle. "What are Peter's long-term objectives?" she asked. "This is a good question to identify Peter's deeper desires and to make him step back from the operational issues and into a better frame of mind to think more strategically and conceptually. Thinking about long-term outcomes rather than focusing only on the issues immediately at hand will also help him see the need to forge alliances and build helpful relationships."

Amanda said, "I didn't get to that point."

"You would have needed to establish rapport first, of course," Lauren affirmed. "It's important to ask him what he wants. What are his aspirations? What does he see as his biggest obstacle to reaching his objectives? You would also need to determine how committed Peter is to change. If he wanted to be the next CEO of the company, he would probably be committed to doing whatever it takes to achieve that goal. But you must first establish a partnership with Peter to help him reach his desired goals."

Lauren thought for a moment. "On second thought," she added, "you, too, need to be aligned with what Peter's objectives are. For example, I was once asked to coach an abrasive leader whose goal was to get her boss fired. She wanted to use my coaching service to help her accomplish it. I refused to coach her with such an objective. I have also declined contracts when the company executives ultimately want to fire the coaching client but are offering coaching first to protect the company's image and guard against charges of wrongful dismissal.

"So remember, if you do not feel any chemistry with a client or are totally misaligned with the leader's or the company's objective, you can refuse to engage in the coaching process. Keep in mind that it's important to first find out what the leader aspires to and how engaged he or she is in reaching that objective. Then find out what your client would need to do to attain his or her coaching goals.

"In Peter's case, also be clear about your assumptions. I assume that if Peter wanted to become CEO of this company, he would need to be better at engaging, empowering, and educating employees. Once you make this clear to him with irrefutable data—given his drive, his Type A personality, and his intelligence—he will be highly motivated to make the needed changes to achieve this long-term objective. This is *my* assumption to date."

"But he has no commitment to change!" protested Amanda. "He tried to fire me. Motivating him to change couldn't possibly be that simple!"

Lauren said, "Before I review your conversation in detail, remember that in the exploratory coaching session, you need to assess clients' strengths, their fears, and the biggest challenges they face in achieving their goals. It is important to make an appraisal of how they learn and what coaching approach will best serve them. Let me make a list of what *you* need to know about Peter to coach him well. Showing your interest in him as a person is a good start in establishing rapport, and it's essential to coaching him successfully."

Coach's Objectives for Understanding the Client After the First Two Sessions

- Client's personal and organizational goals
- Belief system and limiting beliefs
- Commitment to coaching and to change
- Strengths
- Mind-set
- Values
- Assumptions
- Motivation
- Biggest challenges
- Degree of defensiveness
- Ambition
- Fears
- Learning style
- Mental blocks or blind spots
- Incongruities
- Perception of coaching and the coach.

* * *

The Excellent Executive Coaching Process is logical, simple to follow, and adaptable to any coaching situation. It helps the coach form a strong connection with the client early on in the coaching process, which greatly increases the likelihood that coaching will be successful. When you use the Excellent Executive Coaching Process, you'll have clarity about the client's objectives, not just those of key stakeholders, at every step along the way.

It's important to bear in mind that the Excellent Executive Coaching Process is an iterative process, not a linear one. You might not move through the steps in order with each client. The coaching work done during Step 6 (helping the client understand what is holding him or her back) might bring insights that direct you back to Step 3 to formulate a new objective. You should touch on Step 7 at the end of every session. It's not essential to work through the steps sequentially, as long as you are moving with the energy of the coaching process and using that as your guide.

In the next chapter, we'll take a deeper look at Amanda's conversation with Peter, to see what it can teach us about the best ways to handle a difficult or reluctant coaching client.

Chapter Review Questions

1. What are the 10 steps in the Excellent Executive Coaching Process?
2. Is the Excellent Executive Coaching Process linear?
3. What steps, if any, did Amanda cover during her conversation with Peter?
4. What questions should Amanda have asked before she ever met Peter? Of whom?
5. What information should the coach know about the leader after the first and second coaching sessions?

CHAPTER 8

AVOIDING COMMON COACHING MISTAKES

Working With Brilliant and Abrasive Jerks

Now that we've discussed the steps of the Excellent Executive Coaching Process, let's look more closely at the methods a coach can use for directing conversations with a client. In this chapter, we'll take a closer look at Amanda's abortive interaction with Peter and explore the specific mistakes she made and what she might have done

87

differently. As you read, you may recognize missteps you have made in your own coaching practice. In discussing these common coaching errors, the chapter draws on the Excellent Executive Coaching Process, which offers a new way of approaching and interacting with clients that avoids triggering their threat response and helps establish rapport.

Key Tactics for Effective Coaching

- Practice reflective listening and reformulate the client's statements.
- Ask open-ended questions; avoid closed-ended questions whenever possible.
- Let the client introduce the content of the conversation and issues to discuss. The coach should lead the coaching process toward the resolution of those issues. In other words, do not let the client ramble off topic to avoid the issue. Instead, bring the client back to the topic by asking what the link is between his or her rambling and the challenge at hand.
- Clarify how clients define key terms, to avoid misunderstanding.
- Steer the conversation toward positivity when it becomes negative, to maintain the coaching process's energy.
- Use silences after you make a point or ask a question to let the client have time to think. Let the client give you visual eye contact before proceeding with a follow-up question.
- Use a softer tone and speak more slowly when a client is dealing with strong emotions. Leave time for the client to process those emotions. Show empathy, respect, and care without falling into sympathy. When coaches are sympathetic, they lose objectivity and become less helpful to their clients.

* * *

PRACTICE REFLECTIVE LISTENING

As Lauren explored the details of Amanda's failed conversation with Peter, she took care to mix praise in with her criticism.

"You started by telling him that management has decided to offer coaching to all the company's executives," she began. "This has the advantage of being a neutral statement, but it's not the fundamental reason why this particular coaching is taking place. And I'm not sure that it's true. It's never a good idea to lie to your clients."

Amanda replied, "Peter told me up front that he did not want to be coached and did not know why George or John was sending him a coach. What was I supposed to say?"

"Listen to him," Lauren answered. "Reformulate what he just said: 'You have been offered a coach, but you don't know why. Would you prefer talking to John and then decide whether you want to take advantage of coaching?' You caught Peter by surprise. To a person who has little emotional intelligence and is highly focused on results, what you were proposing seemed like a waste of time."

"I told him that all the company's executives were being offered coaching. I thought that would explain it."

Lauren said, "Peter is bright enough to work out that that wasn't the real reason he was being offered coaching. Instead of diplomatically addressing his difficulties, you justified your presence by confronting him about the turnover in his division. Most brilliant, abrasive leaders like to be in control. Not knowing why he is being offered coaching is confusing for Peter. Opening with this approach is unlikely to create rapport. The less connected to you Peter feels, the more likely he is to shift his behavior with you from constructively challenging to intimidating and abrasive." Lauren paused a moment to let Amanda think about that, then continued.

"By approaching Peter too abruptly, without sufficient care to take a neutral stance and avoid seeming like a threat, Amanda, you triggered Peter's fight-or-flight instinct—and, in keeping with his nature as an abrasive leader, his response was to fight. Amanda, you neglected to ensure that Peter felt in control from the very beginning of the coaching process, with predictable results: Instead of a charming, charismatic leader, you were dealing with an angry, aggressive person whose self-protective instincts were on high alert.

"However, Peter is known for being sexist. He probably held his temper back a bit because you're beautiful, and your courage must have amused him. The situation could have been worse." Lauren held back a smile as she spoke.

"In all fairness," she continued, "you were likely already at a disadvantage from the very beginning. As an internal coach, you are a part of Peter's company, but you fall a bit lower on the organizational chart. He likely sees himself as having more power in the company than you do. He might regard it as an insult that upper management sent an 'underling' to deal with him and automatically refuse coaching on those grounds. He might also perceive an internal coach as not having the same rigorous approach to confidentiality that an external coach would have, and if he has any doubt that you could leak confidential information, he is not going to proceed.

"Remember, Peter might fear being perceived as incompetent, which is part of what makes him such a successful, motivated, high achiever. Your suggestion that he would benefit from coaching seems to imply that he is failing in his leadership, which will put him on his guard immediately."

LET THE CLIENT LEAD

"What could I have said if I wanted to convince him to be coached?" Amanda asked.

"It might have been better to do what a researcher does—neutrally collect data by listening to Peter's perception of the situation. After validating what he has achieved, you might have asked something like, 'Do you have any hunches about why you are being offered coaching?' This lets *him* introduce the question of weaknesses and areas where he needs improvement, so he will be less on the defensive.

"If he has no idea or does not want to volunteer information, you could say something like, 'Some key stakeholders are concerned that too many people have left your division. Management has questions about your contribution to these departures. What is your take on the situation?' Peter will probably get defensive. That's okay. Listen to his perspective. Avoid debating what actually happened in his division. The only information you have is hearsay from HR and management."[i]

"That's good advice," Amanda said. "What else could I have done?"

"Stay neutral. Don't take sides about why or how things happened. Say something like, 'I haven't worked for you or your department, so I don't know exactly what happened. I only know there are questions about your leadership style, and these rumors are not good for you. Coaching can help you understand exactly why those rumors surfaced, so that you can create more positive narratives and address negative perceptions that are detrimental to you and your career.'"

When initiating coaching, let the client feel in control. When clients are the ones to suggest areas where they need improvement, they are less likely to go on the defensive.

"I can see that I didn't build the necessary confidence between us to start a coaching process." Amanda said. "Where else did I go wrong?"

"Walk me through the conversation in detail," suggested Lauren. "I'll be able to give you better feedback if I know everything that was said."

---

i Credit for this observation goes to Dr. Laura Crawshaw, who mentioned it to me in conversation in 2005 and later through her Boss Whispering training.

When Amanda had recounted her entire conversation with Peter, Lauren responded, taking care not to offend the younger woman. "You used a lot of closed-ended questions, particularly in the first half of your session."

"What do you mean by closed-ended questions?" Amanda asked, confused.

"Closed-ended questions start with a verb and generally lead to yes or no answers, and they are not conducive to an exploratory conversation. When you ask him questions like, 'Are you achieving your objectives?' Peter can simply answer by a yes or no. He doesn't have to delve any deeper into your question."

"Yes, I see that. I think it's because I was tense."

"It's fine to use closed-ended questions when you want a confirmation that you have understood what's just been said," answered Lauren. "But don't stack one question on top of another. That's bound to come across as aggressive. That's why Peter responded with, 'Is this an interrogation or what?' Your questions came one after another: 'Are you affirmative? Are you assertive when you talk to them? Are you considerate?'

"As you say, asking all those questions in quick succession was a sign that you were nervous, but whatever the reason for it, it's not conducive to creating rapport. It appears that you didn't give Peter time to focus. Ask one well-thought-out question at a time, and wait for the answer. And remember to keep your questions short and to the point. Peter thinks quickly and is impatient. If your questions are too long, before you're halfway through your sentence he'll have guessed what you're trying to say, and he'll stop listening, or he'll start thinking about something else."

Ask clients open-ended questions that invite discussion.

"I guess Peter intimidated me. He has so much gravitas, and he questioned my ability. At one point, I was afraid he might physically attack me. I worried whether I was a good enough coach. I just wasn't able to create any rapport with him."

Lauren responded, "It's not always easy to create rapport with abrasive leaders, but it does help to have empathy for their likely unease with the situation. Peter appears strong because he is uncomfortable showing vulnerability. Who knows, he might perceive you as the police coming on behalf of upper management. How would you feel if you were in Peter's shoes?

"He might also be frustrated at having to take a break from his pressing business activities to talk about people and feelings, which he perceives as a total waste of his time, and he's bound to react badly to that. Stay calm. Being aware of your own performance anxieties is a good start to preventing yourself from becoming defensive. It will help you to refocus your attention on what is best for your client."

"I see," Amanda said. "If I am anxious about my performance, my attention is on *my* actions and behavior instead of on what my client is saying."

*   *   *

Frequently, a coach working with an abrasive jerk may feel a little like Amanda, not sure what to say for fear of triggering an outburst of rage. It's important to keep in mind that for the abrasive jerk, the bluster is often simply a veneer; it exists to cover up vulnerability, uncertainty, and fear of being perceived as incompetent. In other words, *the client is scared, too.* Focus on putting him or her at ease and establishing an understanding between the two of you. You may find that this puts you at ease, too. To prevent your coaching client from mistakenly perceiving you as stupid, keep to the same thinking rhythm as him or her.

If, as the coach, you feel anxious about your own performance, remember that the client is likely anxious, too. Refocus yourself on what the client is feeling and saying, and you may feel more centered.

It's also important, in the initial stages of coaching with a new client, to let the client take the lead. Be careful not to bombard him or her with questions (which can come across as accusatory). Rather, listen carefully to what the client says, and sift those words for clues as to his or her vulnerabilities and thoughts about coaching. Whenever possible, reformulate the client's words and reflect them back to him or her for confirmation. The key is to make clear that you have the client's best interest in mind. Show that you haven't been sent from management to work in opposition to the client, but are there to support and assist him or her. Effective coaching cannot happen until you have won the client's trust and made clear how he or she will benefit from the coaching process.

* * *

Amanda had been listening carefully, taking in all the advice Lauren had given so far. Since Amanda was obviously so deep in thought, Lauren waited a moment instead of jumping back into her analysis. It seemed like a long time before Amanda raised her eyes back to Lauren and asked, "Can an abrasive jerk really change?" she asked. "Even if I could be a perfect coach, it seems like such a stretch."

"Abrasive jerks can come in many forms," Lauren replied. "They fall on a spectrum ranging from decent people with poor interpersonal skills, which can be improved; to self-centered, egotistical manipulators, who are more challenging to help; to psychopaths, who have a chronic mental disorder with abnormal or violent social behavior and need treatment by a mental health professional. It appears that Peter lies between lacking interpersonal skills and being a self-centered manipulator.[ii] Coaching can make the difference."

As Amanda absorbed Lauren's words, she seemed obviously reassured. She asked, "What else could I have improved?"

[ii]   I'm grateful to Simon Langelier for making this point in conversation at https://www.facebook.com/katrina.burrus.

Lauren admired Amanda's eagerness to learn and thought for a moment. "Well, you assumed on several occasions that your definition of a word was the same as Peter's. For example, you didn't explore what Peter meant when he used the words *proactive* and *lethargic*. Instead, you repeated verbatim what he said about his direct reports: 'They aren't proactive.' Here, you missed the opportunity to widen Peter's perspective by exploring the difference between his meaning of the word and yours. So what's your definition of the word *proactive*?"

"*Proactive* is when an employee comes up with a solution in his or her area of expertise," answered Amanda.

Lauren said, "Peter, who is rational, logical, and probably a perfectionist, might interpret *proactive* as being able to write a 'perfect' report that mirrors his own 'impeccable' logic. This is something he finds easy to do but can be a real challenge for some of his direct reports. Or perhaps Peter interprets *proactive* as generating as much business as he does."

"So it's important to define how the client understands terms."

"Yes," affirmed Lauren, "and because Peter has a very high IQ, he has unconscious competence in many areas. He probably assumes that if his direct reports weren't lazy, they would have results similar to his, whether that means developing business or writing brilliant reports. He takes extraordinarily high levels of performance for granted, both for himself and for others. He feels justified focusing on people's flaws because, for him, a flaw is evidence of laziness. If this interpretation underlies the word *proactive*, Peter is making a major assumption that the coach needs to explore and bring to his attention."

"But he's so bright!" Amanda exclaimed. "Why would he make such an assumption?"

Lauren answered, "Certainly he's visionary and bright when restructuring his division, analyzing data, or seeing trends, but he lacks insight into people. Another assumption Peter is likely making is that the same competencies are required for military and organizational leadership. It might have been judicious to get into this a bit more and find out what differences he sees between ideal leadership in the Air Force and in a corporate organization. With this information, you could have helped him uncover his underlying assumptions.

"Instead, you asked about his relationship with his boss. This is a good question in itself, but it has no connection to what Peter had just said about his team. It doesn't build on the prior conversation. The risk with this approach is that you hover on the surface of the many subjects you discuss."

Once again, listening is the key to good coaching. It helps establish a firm base of understanding between yourself and the client, and it lets clients feel that they are in control of the process.

Lauren explained further how a coach might help Peter question and uncover his own assumptions. "When Peter talks about his team members," she said, "it would be good to investigate how he sees each and every one of them—the talents, the core performers, the underachievers, and the ones who have left. How does he perceive them? Have him search for reasons why his direct reports behave the way they do. Don't stick with his first answer. Use the entire floor, as you would if you were dancing the tango.

"Keep encouraging him to see the same situation from different angles. Push for more exploration and self-reflection, but when dancing with your client, let him take the lead. If he starts to become defensive, step back and speak more generally."

"That's a great metaphor," mused Amanda.

"In this case, a good, unthreatening question might be to ask him what type of leadership is effective in a particular situation—which implies that there are different leadership styles to use with different people or circumstances. Then, when he is in a better frame of mind, move forward and push him to reflect on what style of leadership he uses in those circumstances. When your steps are perfectly synchronized and his mind is engaged, introduce a pirouette. Offer a confidential report that only he has access to and that will test his assumptions about how he is perceived by others."

"How do you get him to be in a more conducive state of mind?" asked Amanda. "That seems easier said than done."

Lauren responded, "You might focus Peter's attention on his desired state. It is likely to put him in a better mood. You could compliment him on the achievements he is proud of, but do that only if you are sincere. You don't want him to perceive you as manipulative. You will also find out whether he is open to positive feedback."

Amanda put in, "Because if he can't accept positive feedback, he is unlikely to give it—is that what you are implying? But our conversation went so badly from the start! When could I have given him encouraging feedback?"

"When you asked about the turnover in Peter's division, he responded by telling you what he's achieved since taking over his division. He's quite proud of those achievements.

"He also gave you some information about his concerns, obliquely through his comments about the reductions in his staff. This was a chance to use reflective listening to show him you were paying careful attention to his words and establish a connection between the two of you. You could have shown empathy while reflecting his statements back to him—something like, 'That is quite an accomplishment! I also hear your concern about needing more competent people to sustain those results.'

"You could also have asked him about his long-term goals. This would have given you insightful information about Peter's values and desires," continued Lauren.

Amanda was thoughtful. "I'm beginning to understand why I didn't establish rapport with Peter," she said.

"I empathize with you," affirmed Lauren. "Rapport building can be a challenge. Recently I interviewed eight people who had been badly mistreated by a toxic female manager I was coaching. I heard so much pain and turmoil from them that it began to affect my ability to empathize with the manager. I had to stop the coaching process until I could reconnect with her on neutral ground. Although I empathized deeply with the employees whose careers she had destroyed, I resisted any temptation to moralize my client. Either she was unaware of the impact her behavior had on others, or she was in denial. If I hadn't put my own feelings of injustice in the background, I would have destroyed the rapport I had created with her, which was essential for the coaching process."

"It must have been difficult to remain objective about your client, knowing the awful things she'd done to her employees," sympathized Amanda.

"No," Lauren corrected, "it's not difficult if you keep the entire situation fully in mind. True, the employees had endured a great deal, but their leader was in pain as well. It wasn't hard to feel compassion. The same is true for Peter, you know."

"What? Peter, in pain?" asked Amanda, surprised.

"Yes, Lauren nodded. "Once Peter is no longer in denial, he is likely to feel a great deal of pain."

There was a thoughtful pause while Amanda pondered this.

"Let's get back to your conversation with Peter, Amanda. If we review the second part of your conversation, we see that you shifted to open-ended questions and started to challenge Peter in a positive way. Although you still did not establish the necessary confidence between you, you did appeal to his nature as a results-oriented high achiever when you said, 'What if I told you that I can help you improve your productivity by 30 percent and it wouldn't cost you a dollar?' Here you were focusing on an area where Peter has 20/20 vision and on what motivates him—results.

"When I've worked with Peter in the past, I have noticed he has an unemotional and analytical cognitive style. He is eager to discuss business and results, but, as you know, he has little curiosity about people and feelings. Unfortunately, you presented yourself as being primarily focused on relationships and not being knowledgeable about business. In doing so, you devalued yourself in Peter's eyes and gave him a reason to discount your criticisms. He did this when he said, 'What do you know about business development?'

"Since you hadn't given your credentials earlier, Amanda, you did well not to justify or defend yourself here. Better to refocus Peter's attention on himself and what he can gain. You did this when you told him that working with you would help him leverage his expertise in business development to get even better results." Lauren paused to take another sip of her coffee and let Amanda process all this new information.

* * *

THE COWORKER ACTION RESEARCH REPORT

Abrasive people tend to love hard, credible data and usually have a healthy ego, so it's important to make the client the center of the research focus and to involve people whom the client respects so he or she will value the feedback. In Peter's case, it would be critical to include John

Barbey, the company's CEO, among the interviewed stakeholders, as well as some of Peter's toughest competitors.

Abrasive leaders like Peter rely on exhaustive data to reach business conclusions but often make quick judgments about people. Peter is likely to believe that the coaching process will distract him from getting his "real" work done. The key is to present the issue like a business problem. Enter into the client's mind-set and put the emphasis on what you know is important to him or her. For example, play to abrasive leaders' love of data and their preoccupation with their image by giving them copious reports that only they will have access to.

Presented properly, stakeholder interview reports can serve as a valuable tool to give clients information and a sense of control. The coach should frame the report as practical, concrete business information the client can implement, saying something like, "Once you get some hard data, you decide what you want us to work on." It's critical to put your clients in a decision-making role, as the work of identifying their strengths and weaknesses can be very anxiety provoking. The coaching process can make clients feel powerless, so use the reports to give them back control. As long as the client feels threatened, you won't be able to make any progress in coaching.

A key element of the Excellent Executive Coaching Process is the Coworker Action Research Report, which I developed as an alternative to the popular but flawed 360-Degree Feedback Report (see Chapter 12 for more on the difference between these two reports).[iii] The Coworker Action Research Report is a confidential report, created by the coach and given *only* to the abrasive leader, that summarizes coworkers' perceptions of the leader's strengths and how the leader might adapt his or her

---

iii   Kurt Lewin, then a professor at MIT, first coined the term *action research* in 1944. Action research progresses in a spiral, in which each step "is composed of a circle of planning, action, and fact-finding about the result of the action." Action research is either research initiated to solve an immediate problem or a reflective process of progressive problem solving led by individuals working with others in teams or as part of a "community of practice" to improve the way they address issues and solve problems. (Kurt Lewin, *Resolving Social Conflicts: Selected Papers on Group Dynamics.* Edited by Gertrude W. Lewin. New York: Harper & Row, 1948, pp. 202–203).

leadership to make the relationship with coworkers more productive. How the leader can be more productive might differ with each employee, because people's needs and competencies differ. The focus is on the relationships, with all their intricacies, rather than on the leader's weaknesses.

Because this report is never given to upper management or other key stakeholders without the client's explicit consent, it is less likely than other forms of feedback to trigger instinctive threat responses; accordingly, the leader may be more open to the information contained in the report. It often has a quite eye-opening effect. On the whole, it is generally best to continue meeting with the abrasive leader during the research phase of the report, while coworker interviews are being conducted. This maintains a connection between coach and client and diminishes the leader's apprehension that the coach may lose all positive regard for him or her while gathering the coworkers' feedback. It may also help the coach continue to feel compassion for the abrasive leader's pain.

In compiling the reports, however, the coach must take care to scrupulously follow the proper procedure. The client cannot take part in the process of collecting coworker assessments. Given the sensitive nature of the information coworkers are sharing, all reports must be kept completely anonymous. The abrasive leader's coworkers will likely have painful, emotional stories to tell, and they will feel quite vulnerable doing so; they need to be assured that what they share will remain entirely confidential. At this initial stage of the coaching, an abrasive leader could react to criticism like a cornered rhino ready to attack its prey. Coaching will help rein in this impulse to attack, but in the beginning it's important to protect the leader's coworkers from backlash.

The more abrasive the leader is, the tougher and more brutal the Coworker Action Research Report will be. The abrasive jerks I have worked with are often in denial about their toxic behavior and are therefore surprised and dismayed when they receive such harsh feedback. Abrasive women have broken down and cried. Abrasive men might get choked up or, conversely, claim they knew all along what people thought of them.

Once you have gotten your clients' full attention, reassure them that they *can* change. These brilliant leaders are high achievers with a powerful drive to succeed. When they receive irrefutable proof that their interpersonal behavior is at times intolerable and, what's more, is standing in the way of their success, they are usually convinced to take the bull by the horns and work toward change. And once their mind is made up, these sharp-witted, action-oriented leaders will rise to the challenge with tremendous energy and focus.

Watching this transformation again and again over my years as a coach, I've come to realize that many abrasive jerks do not mean to be diabolical or manipulative but rather are disconnected from emotion and fear being perceived as incompetent.[1] They have a desire for control and a hunger for status. They often lack empathy and emotional intelligence. Their perfectionism and total focus on results blind them to people's feelings and the impact of their behavior on others.

In other cases, abrasive jerks might have been told repeatedly that they have an intimidating and abusive leadership style but find themselves at a loss as to how to change. The Coworker Action Research Report or any other rigorous process (e.g., the Boss Whispering methodology) can offer clients new insights into how they inflict pain on others.[iv] Then and only then can the coaching process help abrasive jerks understand how to

---

iv   The Boss Whispering Institute was founded by Dr. Laura Crawshaw.

control their impulse to attack anyone who doesn't meet their extraordinarily high performance expectations.

* * *

As Amanda listened attentively, Lauren continued to explain the Coworker Action Research Report. "Seeking input from coworkers is essential for understanding the specific issues surrounding the abrasive leader's behavior," she said. "Most 360-Degree Feedback processes include predefined questions that are designed around general statements like, 'His leadership style is abrasive.' But how can you draw up an action plan from that statement? You need specific and detailed feedback that identifies *why* the client's leadership style is perceived as abrasive, such as, 'He often walks three steps ahead of his counterparts, and he rolls his eyes in irritation each time he thinks a comment from his direct reports is below his standard.'

"The research report that you present to the leader should indicate exactly the behavior that he or she *does* that makes people see him or her as abrasive. It's not enough simply to say the leader does not communicate well. For example, does that mean the leader stutters when talking, or that he or she fails to communicate information about strategy changes to direct reports, or does it mean the leader does not walk around the office asking people questions and showing interest in what they are doing? The assessment report needs to be specific and detailed enough to clarify exactly what the leader does that gives a certain perception," added Lauren.

* * *

For the brilliant and abrasive leader to make lasting improvements, the entire system around him or her needs to be involved. As long as coworkers are reacting to the abrasive leader's behavior, rather than doing whatever is in the best interest of the company, everyone connected to the leader inadvertently conspires to perpetuate the abrasive behavior. When abrasive leaders begin to improve their behavior as a result of coaching, they become unpredictable. Suddenly, they are no longer behaving according to the rules their colleagues have become accustomed to. This is unsettling.

When leaders make their first awkward attempts to be more sensitive, their colleagues are likely to perceive these new behaviors as manipulative strategies and think, "Okay, he's being unusually nice, what does he want from me now?" At the beginning of a coaching process, the system around leaders inadvertently pushes them back into their old habits instead of encouraging their initial attempts to change. The best way to avoid this is to ensure that everyone who works with the leader is involved with or knows about the coaching process.

In addition, when abrasive leaders tell people that they are seeking help to improve their behavior, they admit to being vulnerable. This admission humanizes them. Coworkers are more likely to be tolerant and offer encouragement when they see the leader make improvements or even awkward attempts to change his or her behavior. Coaches need to use this system to drive change. For example, Peter's trusted coworkers can provide him with feedback on the spot when he makes notable progress or when he reverts to his old behaviors. If he slips back into his abrasive habits, they can call him on it. These allies can also help the abrasive leader reintegrate more positively into the system.

* * *

Lauren explained this to Amanda, then said, "How coaching is perceived in the company is another good question to ask before the exploratory meeting," Lauren noted. "Coworkers are more likely to act as allies in the process if the concept of coaching is familiar to them, and leaders are more receptive, too. What is the general attitude toward coaching here at Tempus?"

"In our company coaching is not viewed as remedial but as developmental, since many of the top executives receive coaching. But what happens if the company has never offered coaching before?" asked Amanda.

"In that case, coaching probably doesn't have a stigma attached to it. Peter might have been even more defensive if he perceived coaching as only remedial. Some of my Anglo-Saxon clients perceived executive coaching as a perk or a sign of status: 'Look at me, with my big office, my fancy car, and my executive coach.' Some of my clients have proudly presented me to their peers as a sign of accomplishment. Coaching is more likely to be viewed as a perk if it is offered to top management first," added Lauren.

"Conversely," she continued, "executives who see coaching as remedial would never admit to their colleagues that they are undergoing coaching, under any circumstances. These individuals see coaching not as a perk but as a reprimand, or worse. People come to distrust coaching when they see it misused as an excuse to fire the leader, when it is obvious that the key stakeholders are not truly giving the brilliant and abrasive jerk a chance to mend his or her ways.

"For this reason, when you take on a new coaching client, it is important to determine what the stakeholders' true intentions are. Do they really intend to give the abrasive leader a chance to improve? In my experience, stakeholders who say they will give the abrasive leader six months to bring about change often wait only three months to see visible change or wind up firing the leader before even three months have passed."

As she listened, Amanda couldn't help but think how defensive Peter would become if his coworkers were asked to give feedback about him. "Won't Peter be embarrassed if a lot of people in the company know he is being coached about his bad behavior?" she asked. "Won't he be reluctant to have a coach interview his direct reports, peers, and bosses? And what is the coach's responsibility to the client in terms of protecting his privacy?"

"Amanda, it is really important to stay as neutral as possible and collect research data," Lauren answered. "If a respondent asks me a probing question, I am up-front and tell the person that is the type of question I won't answer, because I don't want to influence the respondent's response. Sometimes I even drop my pen, then lean over to pick it up, to hide any response my expression might reveal. Moreover, I do not ask respondents about my client's weaknesses. Instead, I ask about the client's strengths and what would help their relationship be more productive. It sets the responsibility on both of them, so the respondent isn't only finger pointing at the abrasive leader."

If Peter might see coaching as an unexpected punishment and a threat to his privacy, the subject should be approached carefully and diplomatically. Lauren felt that Amanda had failed to do this, with unfortunate results.

She pointed this out to Amanda, saying, "There was one interesting moment when you asked Peter, 'And are you actually getting results?' He might have thought you were calling his results into question, but, surprisingly, his answer showed some vulnerability: 'It's harder now because the economy is lagging.'"

"That's true," pondered Amanda. "He seemed smaller for a moment when he said that."

"Had you asked him to tell you exactly what was harder now, you most likely would have gained some insight into what keeps him up at night. What is his biggest challenge? Where can coaching best support him? Instead, you told him that he's going to be fired. Being fired is the ultimate corporate death sentence. At that point, Peter's anxiety skyrocketed, and you lost that window when he might have opened up to you."

Amanda looked chastened. Lauren continued, "The person who has authority to fire him, and no one else, should be the one to tell him why, under what conditions, and how soon he might be fired if he doesn't make changes. It's management's role to inform him, not yours. I realize that you wanted to call to his attention the seriousness of the situation, but, again, you are a coach, not a manager. Everyone has a specific role to play. However, you could help Peter's bosses to communicate a difficult message to Peter more effectively.

"What happens if the company acquires a new business in Peter's area of responsibility and there is no successor to Peter? Guess what? Peter is likely to be promoted instead of fired. After telling him he was going to be fired, what credibility would you have left then to continue as his coach?"

"None," said Amanda.

"Here's a man who is pulling in 60 percent of his division's revenue. He reorganized the division successfully. It no longer jeopardizes the company's overall profitability. Two division heads failed at the task before Peter took over. He believes he is getting rid of the dead weight within his division by letting go of the people who are lazy and incompetent. And you walk in and tell him he isn't doing a good job! Are you entering into his mind-set to create rapport and begin a conversation where he feels understood?"

Amanda shook her head, embarrassed. Lauren continued, more gently, "Instead of making accusations, find out how he sees things. You could say something like, 'I was told that you are not treating your people well. What's *your* perception of the situation?' Don't put HR in an awkward position."

Just then, there was a knock on the door, and Lauren broke off. Frank looked into the room. "Sorry to interrupt, ladies," he said. "Could I have a word with you, Lauren?"

"Amanda, you have great courage, and I appreciate your willingness to learn," said Lauren. "We'll meet again soon to talk further."

When Amanda had left the room, thanking Lauren and promising to continue their conversation later, Frank perched on the edge of Lauren's desk. "I just talked to Peter," he said. "Would you start a coaching process with him? I think you have a better chance of being successful with him. He knows your reputation for coaching high-profile executives and is impressed."

Lauren tried to hide her smile as she answered, "I would love to." She admired Peter's brilliance. She liked him as a person and understood the pressure he put himself under but also knew how much suffering he caused his colleagues. She looked forward to the challenge of working with this brilliant, abrasive leader.

Chapter Review Questions

1. What type of questions should a coach use for most of the coaching session?
2. Why is it important to define the words a client uses?
3. Where should a coach lead the conversation as soon as possible?
4. What should a coach do if the client is too frustrated to focus on his or her objectives or desired future?
5. Should coworkers be aware of the leader's coaching process? Why?
6. Why should the coach ask whether an organization typically offers coaching to its employees?

CHAPTER 9

COACHING IS SYSTEMIC

*Keeping Management Aware
and Accountable*

Before she could approach Peter about beginning a coaching process, Lauren needed to know exactly where matters stood. Did Peter understand how precarious his position in the company had become? Yes, Amanda had told him his job was at stake, but had he believed her? Lauren had a hunch that Peter might believe he wasn't in any real danger, that he'd upset some oversensitive employees but he had the support of the CEO so, ultimately, he was protected. To find out whether this was true, Lauren needed to speak with Peter's bosses and learn what he had actually been told (Step 2 of the Excellent Executive Coaching Process).

INFORMATION GATHERING IS A TOP-DOWN PROCESS

Lauren decided to begin her information gathering at the top of the organization, by meeting with John. She needed to find out whether John had truly communicated to Peter that if he did not change his behavior he would be fired. She suspected John might have simply told Frank, who told Amanda, and that Peter had not been made fully aware of the consequences he might face for his actions.

Lauren did not have an appointment with John, but she wanted to get started as soon as possible, so the day after her conversation with Amanda, she stopped by his office to ask his secretary, Cindy, whether he was available to see her. When Lauren poked her head around the door, Cindy was on the phone, trying to order sandwiches to be delivered to the office. John had a working lunch coming up in twenty minutes. Cindy looked up at her and, to Lauren's surprise, gave her an understanding nod and waved her in the direction of John's office as she continued giving the lunch order and sifting through papers on her desk.

"What an organized and capable personal assistant," Lauren thought to herself. She was happy to slip in to see John between appointments. Usually Cindy guarded John's schedule with her life.

Lauren knocked on John's door and heard his loud, clear, "Come in." When she entered the room, John was not at his desk; instead, he stood at the window, looking out, once again, at the immense sculpture of the three-legged chair in the middle of the plaza. When he turned and saw Lauren, his face lit up. With a smile, John briskly walked up to her to give her a warm handshake.

"Hello, Lauren, what can I do for you?" he chimed.

Lauren was aware that she only had twenty minutes before John's next appointment. So, without wasting any of that time on small talk, she jumped right in and asked him, "John, have you talked to Peter about the changes you wanted to see in his behavior?"

"Yes," John answered, and his smile disappeared. His facial expression stiffened. "Amanda talked to him about a coaching arrangement. It took me hours to calm him down after that debacle. He was ready to resign. Why in the world did Amanda tell him I would fire him?"

"Yes, I realize that, John. Surely Amanda wanted to highlight for Peter the seriousness of the situation. But what exactly did *you* tell Peter?" asked Lauren.

"I told him that he needed to change his behavior, because more and more work was being done by fewer and fewer people in his division and it was jeopardizing the sustainability of the department," answered John. "Peter simply replied that only the worst performing, laziest, and least competent of the team members had left."

Lauren nodded, unsurprised.

John continued, "Peter was visibly upset. He wanted to know why his behavior was being questioned, given his outstanding results. He then noted that George brings in very few clients and has done nothing to sustain the company's profitability. According to Peter, George's main concern is sending employees to workshops," reported John, clearly annoyed. "Who should I believe? Peter is right. He *is* the best performer. He was employed to restructure the division, and if we lose a few under-performers, that's part of the process of revitalizing a failing department. He's also right about George. I haven't been impressed with his results lately," said John.

Lauren walked closer to John and whispered, as if telling him a secret, "What else did you tell Peter?"

"I told him that he was an outstanding member of our executive team but he needed to improve his behavior and cause less turnover in his division," said John defensively.

"Did you tell him he was going to be fired if he did not change his behavior?" asked Lauren.

"Well . . . not exactly, but I shall do so if I hear of any more resignations on his team. I mentioned this to Frank, but I didn't imagine that he would repeat to Amanda what I told him in confidence."

"Ah," thought Lauren, "it is easy to tell a third party your thoughts but a lot harder to speak your mind face-to-face to the intended person." She persisted, instructing John, "Find out for yourself what people are saying about Peter. Might I suggest that you have lunch in the cafeteria or walk around the departments to inquire how business is being handled in general? Listen to what comes up in the conversation."

Lauren had confidence in John. He would be subtle in his questioning and would not make his investigation obvious, she thought.

When you're gathering information in advance of beginning a coaching process, you may find it necessary to gently push the key stakeholders to give you the full story. In many cases, upper-level managers find it easier to turn a blind eye to the jerk's abrasive behavior because it yields results.

"Yes, I shall find out for myself, " said John with a glance at his watch, visibly annoyed.

Lauren felt his impatience at the thought of having to waste time inquiring about his stellar performer and quickly redirected the conversation. "Does he know I shall be coaching him?" she asked.

"Yes, Peter seemed relieved that his coach was going to be you. I also mentioned that you would be coaching other key members of the executive committee and that this was a developmental process, not a remedial one."

"Hmm," thought Lauren. John had not told Peter in explicit terms that his job was in jeopardy. She assumed that John thought Peter's behavior was situational and caused by the need to restructure his division. Lauren now understood why Peter did not comprehend the severity of his situation.

But why did John tell Frank he was going to fire Peter if he saw no change in his leadership? Peter obviously thought he was doing well, given his outstanding results, and he was getting mixed messages from John, thought Lauren with frustration as she left John's office. She could hear John's lunch guest in the hall having a flirtatious conversation with Cindy, and she knew her brief audience with John was over.

But, with one hand on the doorknob, Lauren suddenly stopped short and said quietly, so as not to be heard by the guest just outside the door, "One quick question, John: What are Peter's leadership strengths, and what would make your relationship with him more productive? Let us start with his strengths." Lauren gently closed the door and walked back toward John's desk.

With confidence, John said, "Peter's strengths are numerous. He is incredibly professional, with a phenomenal workload capacity. He is devoted to the company's clients and products. His clients love him. He is charming socially and dedicated to me. However, I am told he is abrasive with his team."

"What else?" Lauren asked.

"Peter is used to working on his own in difficult, emerging markets. He is used to crisis situations and has been hired on several occasions to sort out serious problems." John thought for a moment and continued, "He likes to work independently and force issues through. I have no problems with him personally. On the contrary, we get along very well. And his clients love him."

"Good," Lauren said. "Does anything else come to mind?"

"He might lack flexibility. I am told his interpersonal radar is broken and he does not easily receive social cues, but you must remember, Peter's division has a five-year history of being badly managed in China, and, in all fairness, his brief for this job was to be in charge and make it work. He has done an outstanding job. His style might be too confrontational and aggressive for the Asian market, but he gets things done. He has a 'can-do' attitude."

Lauren interrupted John, seizing the opportunity to dive in and find out precisely how aware John was of Peter's negative behavior by restating John's words. "How, specifically, do you know that his style does not work with his employees? Give me a concrete example, John."

John cleared his throat and said, "Apparently, many of his employees do not carry out orders. They will only deal with him through emails. This situation makes him even more aggressive with them. Others are devoted to him and will work endlessly on weekends and during vacation time just to please him. Peter has his in-group and an out-group. But how much more can he stretch and overextend the in-group?" questioned John.

"You're right, Lauren, I shall have to go to his division and see for myself how he is perceived. I'll get back to you tomorrow, but now, if you will excuse me, I need to attend to my next appointment," said John as he opened his door to warmly greet his next guest.

> During the information-gathering process, there are two key questions to ask of stakeholders: "What are the leader's strengths?" and "What would make your relationship with the leader more productive?"

He escorted Lauren out the door with a "See you tomorrow," accompanied by a gracious smile. John had a way of making you feel that you were the most important person in the world, even when he was seeing you out the door and visibly strained.

"Now, how does he do that?" Lauren wondered. "I will have to observe what he *says* and *does* that gives you this feeling that you are so important. Maybe Peter can learn something from John's technique. Since Peter respects John so much, he might like to emulate John and maybe would even agree to learn from him."

Before leaving, Lauren stopped briefly at Cindy's desk to schedule another appointment for the following day. She caught a quick glance pass between Cindy and John before he greeted his next appointment. They must have had a secret code between them, because Cindy readily booked Lauren for the following day. It usually took a month to get a one-on-one meeting with John, outside the weekly executive committee meetings. Obviously, he wanted to get to the bottom of this situation. It was troubling him.

* * *

The next day was beautiful, with the smell of spring in the air, and after lunch with a friend, Lauren was relaxed and happy that Peter's coaching was finally going to take place. She ambled through John's open door at the prescribed time of their appointment. She found him at his desk. He had a severe expression and was obviously upset. Lauren had barely sat down in the chair he pointed to when he started speaking.

"I am going to restructure Peter's division and take his team away from him," John said grimly. "He will no longer be responsible for the global commercial development of Asia. He is gifted in finance, so he can take over that expert function and not have any real management responsibility at all."

Surprised, Lauren interrupted, "You are going to remove his responsibilities, restructure the division, and eliminate his interaction with his team? How is isolating him going to resolve the problem?" She was taken aback that John had shifted so quickly from viewing Peter as his protégé to wanting to demote him from management and keep him from interacting with others.

John was quick to answer. "I took your suggestion, Lauren. Yesterday afternoon I spent some time walking through the departments and talking with people. I went to the cafeteria for my coffee this morning instead of having Cindy bring it to me. You were right, I learned a lot—and none of it was good."

Lauren sighed, although she wasn't terribly surprised. "Tell me what you learned," she said.

"There is a mutiny against him in the IT department, Peter's out-group is passively resisting him, and his in-group is overworked. I would not be surprised if at least one of the employees in his in-group burns out in the next few months."

"A mutiny?" Lauren broke in with surprise.

"Apparently when Peter was away on vacation last month, they realized that all the tension in the division was suddenly gone. He'd been putting enormous pressure on them to perform, to make his own division look good. They told me that their entire department would resign en masse if Peter's behavior wasn't addressed. I can't have this! People are tiptoeing around him. They fear him. So tell Peter that if he doesn't change, he will have to go."

"No," Lauren sighed. "John, you are his boss, and he respects you. It is important that you tell him, as his line manager, and, furthermore, it will have a lot more impact if you are the one to speak to him, rather than a peer like me. And before you make this sudden decision, remember all the positive qualities you listed just yesterday. In many ways he is excellent at his job."

"But you can't change a zebra's stripes," John snapped uncharacteristically, obviously upset that Peter had failed to live up to all the promise John had seen in him. Lauren could even see a flicker of pain pass in his eyes. From the stern look on his face, Lauren presumed that he was seriously considering firing Peter, not just demoting him, although she kept that observation to herself.

"If he were to change his ways, would you keep him?" Lauren asked gently.

"Yes," was John's quick reply. "He is an outstanding performer, and I feel indebted to him for turning his division around."

After a moment's thought, he said, "But I don't see that happening. As a matter of fact, I am now considering firing Peter. The complaints I heard are not acceptable from a senior leader in our company. Why was I not aware of this?"

Lauren was about to suggest a reason, when he interrupted her. "There is no collaboration between George and Peter's division. Employees are reacting according to Peter's mood instead of what is best for the company. I cannot have this. Peter has his in-group devotees, but they are just a minority of the people on his team. Many passively resist Peter's endeavors.

"I learned this morning that a few days ago Peter was in a rage against one of his direct reports," John continued. He took his employee's mobile and threw it across the room, where it broke into a million pieces. We cannot have this behavior from our employees, much less from one of our leaders," he exclaimed.

Lauren interrupted, "You are right, John. This behavior is unacceptable and against the company's leadership principles. However, you promised Peter a leadership development and coaching program. He is a key performer. If you isolate him, you won't be making use of his strengths—the skills that got his division out of the red. Do you really think that isolating

Peter and restructuring the division is the best option for the company?" asked Lauren.

"If you move him to another department, John, you are actually just displacing the problem. Peter is intelligent, and if we present him with irrefutable data that his behavior is not conducive to his success, he will come to realize the harm he's doing and want to change his ways."

"But once he knows the effect of his behavior, will he change?" asked John.

"No" said Lauren, "not immediately. After he gains insight, he will need to learn new behaviors. Coaching will assist him in trying out these new behaviors. Remember, we all have faults that we are unaware of. It is just that Peter's blind area is his interpersonal relationships. He is brilliant cognitively but less astute in connecting with others."

"You mean he is too self-centered and ego driven," interrupted John.

"I believe Peter is unaware or in denial of his destructive ways," interjected Lauren. "Once he gains awareness and forms a clear understanding of how he can be both results oriented *and* interpersonally savvy, he will change his ways. It is in his interest."

"Won't the change last only as long as we put pressure on him?" asked John.

"Once Peter gains insight, he won't be quite the same, but he also needs time to integrate the new behaviors into his repertoire," said Lauren. "If he does not change, you can always let him go, but at least you will have given him a chance to develop collaborative skills."

"Ok," John decided. "I'll give you six months to show me that Peter can change, but if the coaching doesn't produce the desired change in his behavior, then I shall restructure the division so that he can do no harm, or else fire him, and it would be much to my regret."

Lauren knew from experience that if John said she had six months to prove the effectiveness of her leadership development coaching program, in fact, she really only had three months at the most.

"John, if he does change his ways, will you leave him in his current position? And what potential does he have to evolve within the company if he becomes the ideal leader?" Lauren needed to know Peter's potential to grow within the company if he really transformed his interpersonal behavior.

"Peter is a stellar performer, results-wise. He could be the next CEO, but I just cannot let him or anybody else treat people the way he does. It is unacceptable. Frankly, I am shocked by the feedback I received. You have six months for Peter to show visible change and positive leadership behavior, not a day more."

"Thank you, John."

Lauren was satisfied with the way her conversation with John had gone. Given the influence corporate culture has on employees' perception of acceptable behavior, she knew that no real progress could be made until the company's CEO came to understand the damage Peter's abrasive approach was doing. She had finally succeeded in getting John to look past the big picture—the positive results Peter was getting and the improvements he'd made in the company—to see that in the details of interpersonal behavior, a lot of harm was being done. Now that John was convinced of the need for true change, Lauren was cautiously optimistic that not just Peter but the corporate culture as a whole could start on a new and better path.

The next step would be to speak with George, Peter's immediate boss. Lauren expected this conversation to be a little more difficult, given how angry George was and how close to burnout he'd been the last few times she'd spoken with him. Still, she was confident that she could work with him to get the results she needed.

INVESTIGATING THE MANAGER–COACHEE RELATIONSHIP

What Is George's Perception of Peter?

A few hours after her meeting with John, Lauren tapped on George's office door and poked her head in. It was late, after 6:30pm, and most of Tempus's employees had gone home already, but she knew George would still be working. "George, do you have a minute?" she said. "I was just stepping out for a coffee, do you want to join me?"

George lifted his head slowly to look at her. "Okay," he answered with an exhausted sigh.

George did not utter a word on the way to the company canteen. At the coffee machine, he made himself a double espresso. The canteen was deserted this late in the day, and they settled in a discreet corner, out of sight of anyone who might stroll in. Lauren searched George's face for any signs of his emotional state. His expression was tense, and there were dark circles under his eyes. His clothes looked as if he had slept in them the night before. Flopping down in his chair, he sighed and fumbled in his pocket for a cigarette, before realizing he couldn't smoke in the office.

Lauren interrupted the heavy silence, saying softly, "You've probably guessed that I wanted to talk with you about Peter. Could you tell me more about how you see him?"

With another deep sigh, George answered, "Peter has a mercurial temperament. In meetings he can conduct himself in a very professional manner, drawing on exhaustive data and careful analysis when making decisions—then suddenly, when he feels that his status or opinion has been challenged, he loses his composure. He starts belittling the team member who has bruised his ego. He uses humiliation, sarcasm, and finger pointing to denigrate his opponents. He alienates people!"

George paused, took a sip of his coffee, and continued. "He constantly usurps my authority by going to John every time he wants something or when I ask him to do something he disagrees with. He makes a case to John for why he should go ahead with his own plan in spite of my refusal, John concedes, and I feel like I have no influence at all."

"Have you spoken to John about the consequences his behavior has for your relationship with Peter?" Lauren asked softly.

"No!" George shouted. "John protects Peter. He is a high producer, and he has specialized, expert knowledge in finance. Since Peter turned around the division, John has been back in the good graces of the board of executives. He has a special interest in keeping Peter happy—that is, as long as Peter's results are exceptional.

"Peter is toxic with his direct reports, but I have noticed he clams up in the presence of John and becomes almost subservient. He is not in his comfort zone working with John. He wants John's approval—his fatherly approval, I might almost say.

"John does not realize that his tolerance of Peter's toxic behavior discourages team members from coming forth and offering ideas," George continued. "Team members no longer collaborate. Peter pits one against the other."

What Has George Already Tried?

Now that George had been given a chance to vent and release some of his pent-up tension, it was time for Lauren to move on to the real purpose of the conversation: information gathering. "How have you tried to address Peter's negative behavior?" she asked.

George blurted out, "I've tried everything. I told him he needed to change his behavior toward his employees. I insisted that he attend an emotional intelligence and interpersonal development workshop. Peter flatly declined. He said he had more important things to do, like getting new clients, and maybe I should follow his example and start doing what I was paid to do. He told me I was wasting my time working on talent management, that was HR's responsibility, and we don't have time for that kind of soft touch. I insisted that he should go to the interpersonal development workshop, and, I have to admit, I started shouting at him that we could not afford to lose any more employees. And what do you think was Peter's reaction?"

Lauren looked at George expectantly, waiting for him to continue.

"He went to John to discuss an important deal that he was in a good position to close. Peter is clever. He knows how to approach a difficult situation and get what he wants. He then mentioned that I had asked him to attend a workshop on developing interpersonal relationships. I heard that Peter even said I should attend the course instead, because I don't close half as many deals as Peter does. John laughed and told him he might be right. John is diminishing my authority without even realizing it." Looking embarrassed, George swallowed the rest of his coffee in one go. "Peter bypasses me and goes to John whenever he wants something."

Lauren placed her hand softly on George's arm. She could see how frustrated and discouraged he was. She said quietly, "From my perspective, and I may be wrong, Peter tends to see any problem as being caused by the other person's attitudes and behaviors, not his own. Because he is professionally successful, his current behavior has been reinforced over time. He sees no reason to change. In fact, he might actually attribute his success in part to his behavior."

George, who had been gazing into the distance in silence, suddenly looked at Lauren intensely. "John gets along very well with Peter and is grateful for his impressive results. He is almost fatherly toward Peter. He even admires Peter for being tough and direct. John is a very gracious man with a high IQ and a lot of interpersonal savvy. Because Peter is only abrasive with people who don't have power over him, John isn't fully aware of it. Peter is manipulative and calculated, but he's subservient to John and charming to the board members and key clients."

When you speak with people who are particularly frustrated or discouraged by the abrasive leader's behavior, give them a chance to vent before you try to gather real information.

At this point, Lauren decided it was time to interrupt George's grievances and take the opportunity to ask him several questions to start gathering data for the Coworker Action Research Report. "George," she said, "what are Peter's strengths, and what would make your relationship with him more productive?"

George paused, staring into his coffee cup as if searching for answers there. Finally, he acknowledged, "Peter is committed to doing his best. He is smart and has an uncanny ability to identify what might go wrong. He backs up his arguments with irrefutable data. He has an outstanding knowledge of commerce and understands brands. He brings good ideas to the table, but now that I think of it, he lacks confidence. He might stay silent in a meeting with John but then suddenly make an incisive remark. If he stopped at that, he would be a remarkable contributor to the team's dynamics, but it is obvious that he wants to impress on people that he is bright and that without him, Tempus would be in a worse state.

"When he encounters resistance, he becomes aggressive, hierarchical, very top-down. He stops collaborating with people of different opinions and devalues the contributions of employees with less stature. Although he's bright, he is emotionally blind. We depend on him for our success in the Asian market. But he has little to no empathy or social radar. He lacks sensitivity to other people's needs. And he does not know how to pitch himself to engage people who don't see him as a mentor."

Lauren noted wryly that even when he began by listing Peter's positive qualities, George couldn't help eventually coming back to criticism and frustration. She broke in, "How will you know that Peter's coaching is successful, George? How will you measure his progress? What will you be looking for?"

George gave the question some thought and said, "The Asia region, instead of resisting him, would want to work with him. He would be less of a loner and less isolated. He would integrate his out-group and get them to follow him.

"I will know that Peter has changed when everyone around him is positive about him. When he does not alienate people or always draw the glory to himself. For me, he will succeed when he is able to develop talent and bring people up and forward. When his *people* succeed. Peter is so smart, but he uses much of his intelligence to bring everything back to him. He wants you to think, 'Thank God he is here to save the company.'

"Lauren, if I had to put it into one sentence, I would say the 'success criteria' would be reached when I hear Peter say, 'Wow, I am amazed by the people and talent in this region. They are doing a phenomenal job.' Ha! That would be the day!"

Lauren smiled. "Anything else?"

"I am dependent on Peter to bring out the best in people. We need our global teams to collaborate and communicate well with each other. He should be less pushy and better at pulling people toward him. If only he could learn to take a back seat and let his people play the main role. But he has an 'everything is down to me' attitude."

Lauren read the expression of discouragement on George's face. She wanted to hug him, but instead she gently squeezed his arm, smiled, and said, "I am here if you want to talk."

George gave her a sad smile and said, "Lauren, I won't think less of you if you are not able to change Peter. To be truthful, I doubt he *can* change."

Lauren answered, "Indeed, I cannot change Peter if he does not want to change. He has to decide he wants to change his ways. I cannot make the changes for him. So I shall need to bring Peter convincing data showing him that his methods are actually preventing him from getting what he wants. However, he also needs to receive a clear message from you and

John that you expect him to change his behaviors and what the consequences will be if he fails to do so," said Lauren.

Suddenly George perked up. "Did he accept the coaching? I heard that he refused Amanda and her coaching attempts were a fiasco. Peter went to John after his meeting with Amanda and threatened to resign."

"Yes, yes, I am aware," said Lauren, hoping George would not start venting his frustration again.

"In my opinion, that would have been the best solution." George paused, considering, then continued. "What happens if he doesn't accept the coaching? Should we force him to undergo a coaching process?"

Lauren interjected, "George, coaching is voluntary. If he does not accept the coaching, that is his right. Coaching cannot be forced on him. However, if his behavior does not improve, then the company can take disciplinary action."

"You mean fire him or isolate him," interrupted George. "Peter is too expensive to be working as a specialist in isolation, and transferring him to another department just shifts the problem elsewhere. It doesn't address his toxic behavior, does it?"

"You're absolutely right," agreed Lauren.

"Lauren, realistically, Peter couldn't change even if he wanted to," groaned George. "He is a full-grown forty-year-old. It's too late for him to change his ways."

"Have a little faith," Lauren told him with a smile. "I have a feeling I might be able to make some progress with him."

As she said goodnight to George and left the canteen to gather her things and head home for the night, Lauren was filled with empathy for the discouraged, frustrated, nearly defeated man she had been speaking with for the last hour. But she was pleased with the day's work and felt that with the information she had gathered, she was poised to make some significant progress with Peter.

Chapter Review Questions

1. In what ways did it benefit John to overlook the full extent of Peter's abrasive behavior?
2. What was Lauren trying to make John realize and do?
3. Why did she think demoting Peter to an expert role without management responsibilities was not a solution?
4. What useful information did Lauren gather when talking to George?
5. What step in the Excellent Executive Coaching Process is Lauren undertaking here?

Chapter 10

Let the Client Lead

Convincing an Abrasive Jerk to Start a Coaching Process

Given that the situation with Peter had become untenable, as Lauren's conversation with George had revealed to her, she wasted no time getting in touch with Peter. She arrived at the office the next morning with coffee cup in hand, eager to talk to him and see what they could accomplish together. Instead of having her secretary schedule an appointment, she thought it best to personally give Peter a call to find an opportunity to connect with him and test the waters. Lifting the receiver, she dialed Peter's number.

"Yes," he answered in a rough and rapid manner.

"Hi, Peter, this is Lauren. I'd like a few moments of your time when it's convenient for you. When can we meet?"

"Now," he answered curtly, as if he was ordering her in his office immediately.

"Okay, I'm on my way," answered Lauren, already up and ready to go before she put the receiver down. "Well," she thought to herself. "Peter must have talked to John and wants to quickly get to the root cause of the problem." Lauren was glad Peter was action driven. It was a good omen.

Let the Client Lead

Heading straight to Peter's office, she knocked on his door and walked in. She could sense he was observing her every move, with special attention to her long legs, the curve of her hips in her black pencil skirt, and her high-heeled pumps. Obviously he liked women. It made her uncomfortable, but she ignored it, unwilling to play into his seductive power dynamics.

"What's up, Lauren?" he asked brusquely, continuing to watch her with that assessing gaze.

"Mmm," thought Lauren, "I should have asked John to tell Peter to call me instead of making the first move."

Abrasive leaders tend to be more responsive if they are the one to initiate an interaction, because this avoids putting them on the defensive. Lauren felt slightly at a disadvantage being the one who had to speak first. But, on second thought, she realized, if she had let him make the first move, she might have had to wait longer than she wanted to get a meeting scheduled.

If possible, arrange things so that the abrasive leader makes the first move before coaching is initiated. This will give the leader a sense of control and avoid putting him or her on the defensive.

Now Lauren had the delicate job of ensuring that Peter did not perceive her as a predator *or* as his prey. She doubted he would see her as a predator, as Peter took a dim view of coaching and of human resources in general, seeing it as an overemotional waste of time and well below the revenue-generating work that he did.

Determined not to be perceived as prey, she strode into his office with confidence, leveled her gaze to his, steadied her voice, and smiled charmingly. She was going to use all the competitive advantage of being a woman to charm and slightly destabilize him. Smiling genuinely at him was also easy, as she sincerely liked and admired Peter for his incisive mind and had never had any problem with him in the past.

"What's up, Lauren?" asked Peter again. Obviously, he was not going to bring up the subject of coaching.

Lauren tried to get the conversation going. "Well, John asked me to come and see you, Peter. Do you know what it concerns?"

She deliberately matched her tone of voice to Peter's, then waited in silence for him to reply. As she waited, she adopted his posture as much as she could without mimicking him or looking oddly masculine. Lauren knew that surreptitiously imitating Peter's nonverbal communication might help establish a trusting relationship more rapidly. Mirroring can encourage people to let their guard down, because they feel they are speaking with someone who's familiar and similar to them.[i]

Mirroring the client's nonverbal signals and body language can help build rapport quickly, without the client even noticing.

---

i   The theory of neuro-linguistic programming proposes that synchronizing one's voice, body, posture, and other nonverbal signals with the coachee's, while maintaining an open posture, helps establish a trusting relationship more rapidly. Coachees gain confidence when they recognize themselves in the coach. (Krisztina Fazekas, "What Exactly Is Neuro-Linguistic Programming [NLP]? & How Does the Media Use it on Us?" From the Collective Evolution website: http://www.collective-evolution.com/2015/02/10/what-exactly-is-neuro-linguistic-programming-nlp-and-how-does-the-media-use-it-on-us/.)

She was not going to be the first to talk or justify why she was in Peter's office; she refused to give him the upper hand. Instead, she sat in silence and looked at him expectantly.

"Well . . ." said Peter, after what seemed like an endless silence.

"Well, yes," answered Lauren softly, bending forward in her chair as if she were expecting to hear a secret.

"You know, Lauren, I am this company's biggest income generator . . ." Peter paused. He was lost in his thoughts.

Be a Neutral Observer

Lauren waited to see whether Peter was going to continue talking, but he stayed silent, so, to reassure him, she affirmed, "Yes, you have done an outstanding job of turning around your division, which would otherwise have drained this company into bankruptcy. It is quite an accomplishment."

With these words, she could see his body relax a little more and his voice soften. Peter leaned forward in his chair, drawing closer to her. She could see that his apprehension was subsiding and his curiosity with regard to her had increased.

By refusing to open the conversation with criticism or a problem she had been sent to solve, Lauren had avoided putting Peter too much on the defensive. She'd used mirroring techniques to put him even further at ease, matching her posture and other nonverbal signals to his as much as possible. Now, with her admiring comments about the work he had accomplished, she had shown herself to be on Peter's side and made it clear that she was not a threat. Although she hadn't won him over quite yet, he hadn't thrown her out of his office, the way he had with Amanda.

"Yes, Lauren, but some less productive members of the company think I am too rough on them, and John is concerned. But you must understand, I cannot stand people who are lazy and stupid. I think the company is better off getting rid of them. I proved my point. Tempus has done really well ever since I took over the division. I don't understand why John should be bothered. I have been working day and night for this company," continued Peter, reassuring himself.

"Yes, that might be the case." Lauren was not going to argue with him. He was still on the defensive. The questioning tone of her voice just left a slight doubt as to whether she was agreeing with him.

"Well, what do you think, Lauren?" asked Peter.

She was not going to be drawn into a battle of facts or opinions. Peter was such a logical, quick-thinking, competitive man that if they began to debate the issue, he would never back down until he had won.

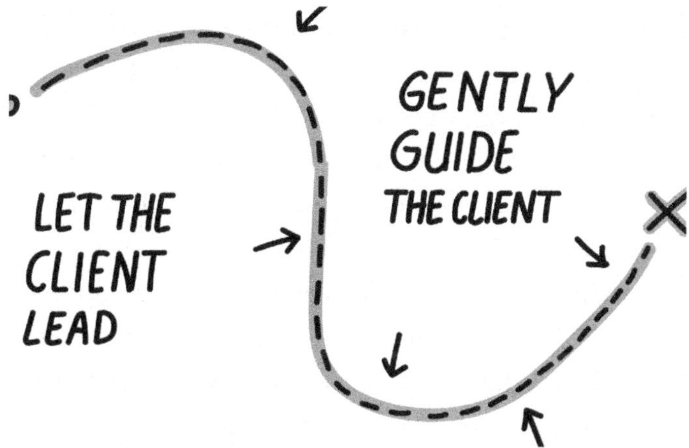

"I don't know, Peter. I don't know the people who work for you well enough to judge," she answered softly. "I know you have produced extraordinary results and you have worked night and day to achieve them," she said sincerely.

"John is concerned that there has been a lot of turnover in my division, leaving more work to be done by fewer people, and he thinks I should be coached," continued Peter, visibly concerned about John's opinion of him.

"Well, what do *you* think, Peter?" interjected Lauren.

"As I said, I disagree."

Peter's body started stiffening again. Lauren backed off. She needed to energize the conversation with positivity.

"Yes, you disagree," she said. Knowing that Peter protected and defended his core in-group, Lauren asked, "What about the employees who have remained in your division, Peter? What standards do they have?"

Gently and with sincere interest, Lauren tried to discover Peter's values and criteria of excellence. She had found that a leader's values usually explain much of his or her behavior. Peter valued results, to the detriment of other important characteristics, such as honesty and interpersonal relationships. His drive for success and achievement explained many of his behaviors, and it made sense that he would react strongly to anyone who impeded his progress.

People strive for the things they value as criteria of excellence, and if they or others fall short of these criteria, they may be disappointed (or become aggressive, in the case of an abrasive jerk). Abrasive jerks may also project their shortcomings onto others with regard to their criteria of excellence. In Peter's case, it is most important to identify what he is striving for consciously or unconsciously, because that will be his motivation to change his behaviors and his drive to make all the necessary efforts.

"They are my best assets. We can achieve the same results with fewer team members," continued Peter. "It puts a little more strain on them, but they can do it. The human resources department has hired some less-than-stellar performers—but those people are gone now," Peter said with a defiant look at Lauren. "If the HR department had done a more thorough job researching the candidates' background, I wouldn't be in this situation." He glanced down at his agenda with a concerned look on his face.

"Hmm, does he really believe what he is saying?" thought Lauren. Peter had been part of the hiring process for all his direct reports. Yet it was no surprise to her that he denied having any role in the problem. She saw beyond his words: He was sincerely concerned about his remaining team members but denied any responsibility.

LET THE CLIENT INTRODUCE THE PROBLEM

Lauren needed to pick up on a problem that Peter had mentioned on his own, so that she could explore it with him delicately but also use it to introduce the idea of coaching. So she said to Peter, "You mentioned that your current direct reports might be under some strain, because they are such high achievers and you have a lower head count in your department now. You also mentioned that John is concerned you are too rough on your direct reports.

"What we could do is find out whether your direct reports are experiencing any strain and whether your core group perceives your leadership as tough. We could also ask them what beneficial qualities you have as a leader, of course. You want to leverage your strengths. You have achieved good results through your leadership assets, but let's find out whether there is any issue or perception that might overshadow your incredible accomplishments. That would be a pity.

"It would be a courageous act on your part to ask for feedback from your boss, peers, and direct reports. Many people don't have the courage. Do you think you are up to it?" asked Lauren, knowing full well that there is nothing quite as effective as challenging a high achiever.

Lauren's approach had been carefully calibrated. She used as her entry point a problem that Peter had introduced on his own—John's concerns that Peter was too hard on his employees—and offered to help him resolve that problem. She framed the suggestion that she would talk to his direct reports about his leadership as a means of improving his impressive results even more—leveraging his strengths. A logical, results-driven man like Peter might be convinced by the offer of a workable solution to one of his biggest problems. And by framing the approach as a matter of courage and as a challenge, Lauren had thrown down a gauntlet for Peter to pick up. Now, she wondered, would he bite the bait, or was it too early to tackle the subject?

Abrasive leaders are typically highly competitive and achievement-oriented. Framing the coaching process as a challenge or a way to solve a problem they have mentioned may be very effective.

"Who would you ask to participate, and what is the process?" asked Peter.

"It's called the Coworker Action Research Report. We'll include people you respect and who can give you the best information about your leadership. Remember, you are the only one who will receive the feedback, and we want to know whether your direct reports feel strained and whether there are any negative perceptions about your leadership that might hinder your career. We also want to know your leadership strengths, as I mentioned."

Offer the Client Hard Data and Feedback

Lauren knew that for Peter to truly listen to the feedback, he needed to respect the people who were part of the research inquiry. He needed to select the key stakeholders himself, so that he felt he was an integral part of the process. It would also give him more control, which would diminish any potential anxiety about the process. He would likely choose the employees with whom he had the best working relationship, which would put him more at ease about the feedback he would receive and help him feel less threatened by the process.

"I would suggest you include your boss, your peers and direct reports, and anyone else whose feedback you consider important, such as customers, family, or friends," continued Lauren, wanting to get Peter's full attention.

"How many stakeholders do you need?" asked Peter.

"About ten to twelve respondents," answered Lauren. "For anonymity's sake, after you select eight interviewees, I will add a couple more respondents to your list. Keeping the respondents anonymous allows them to really share what they think, and we want a crystal-clear view of the situation so that you can then decide which perceptions you want to change and which ones you want to leverage."

By framing the additional interviewees as "a couple more" just for anonymity's sake, Lauren had managed to deftly ensure that the interviews include more critical feedback, without arousing Peter's defensive threat response.

"Remember, Peter, you are the only one to receive this information," Lauren added with conviction. "I want you to get a full and reliable picture of how you are perceived."

Peter didn't respond, but it was clear she had his attention.

"In my experience," she continued, "I have found that a number of the people who participate in this process end up coming directly to you to discuss what they disclosed in the interview, so be prepared to open your door if they come to talk to you, and be sure to listen to them without justifying your position or actions.

"You can agree or disagree with the stakeholders' advice, but instead of responding immediately, reformulate what they said and reflect it back to them so that they feel listened to. You can always explain the reasons behind your actions later, but if you do it then and there, it will appear as if you're not truly listening to them. If you want, we can discuss people's reactions later and determine what would be the most strategic way to respond."

Let the client know that some stakeholders may approach the client directly after their Coworker Action Research Report interview. Reinforce that this is a time to listen without responding defensively.

Lauren used the word *strategic* on purpose, because Peter had mentioned over coffee the other day that strategy was one of his favorite aspects of his job, and one he saw as very important.

"What would you ask them in the interview, Lauren?" interrupted Peter.

"Let me explain the Excellent Executive Coaching Process first and how the questions fit in," suggested Lauren. Using the whiteboard hanging on the wall across from Peter's desk, Lauren sketched out her coaching process, as well as the steps of the Coworker Action Research Report.

Coworker Action Research Report: Interview Process

Preparing for the Interviews

1. Ask the client to compile the list of respected interviewees he or she wants feedback from.
2. Add two to four anonymous stakeholders (e.g., new employees, customers) to the list, with input from HR or the client's boss if need be.
3. Reassure the coaching client (verbally and in the coaching agreement) that no one else will see the report.

Conducting the Interviews

1. Schedule stakeholder interviews.
2. Repeat at each interview that the information is confidential and identifying material will be removed.
3. Let respondents know they may add or delete information later if they choose.
4. Interview stakeholders until the information from the interviews becomes redundant.
5. Identify the client's protectors and defenders.
6. Review the interviews to compile observations about the client's leadership behaviors.
7. Regroup similar observations into patterns or categories.
8. Delete any identifying material.
9. At the end of the interview, inform stakeholders that the client's progress might be awkward and nonlinear in the beginning, and coach them about how to help the client improve.

Lauren and Peter discussed the steps of the process together, then she brought the conversation back to the immediate issue. "You don't necessarily need to follow your stakeholders' suggestions," she said, "but, yes, it is important that you thank participants and start a dialogue. I would facilitate the initial conversation to leverage learning between you and your key stakeholders. For the relationship to be most productive, you need a two-way dialogue that should last well beyond your coaching. Remember, you learn from your stakeholders, and they from you," clarified Lauren.

Peter nodded in understanding.

"The two questions I would ask the stakeholders you selected are, 'What are Peter's qualities as a leader?' and 'What would make your relationship with Peter more productive?'" Lauren then handed some of the control back to Peter, inquiring, "Is there any other question you would want me to ask them?"

"No," Peter said quietly, looking over the steps Lauren had written on the whiteboard.

FOCUS ON THE CLIENT'S GOALS AND OBJECTIVES

"You have achieved outstanding results in your time with Tempus," Lauren continued. "If stakeholders feel your leadership is tough, let us see whether that toughness is overshadowing your excellent results or serving as a deterrent to your long-term goals. If that turns out to be the case, we can work together to change whatever might be detracting from your success. May I ask you where you want to be in two to three years?" probed Lauren.

Peter paused a moment to think, then said slowly but with increasing excitement, "I want to put the Asian market on the map. I love the challenge of developing markets. I want fine watches to be more desirable in Asia than in Europe. I want to leave behind a very experienced and driven team that is not only functionally oriented but business savvy, full of innovative ideas, and equipped with a clear overview of the business.

"Asia is still fragmented. Managers in China have less experience than I do. I want to leave them with my experience. I want to get my department and the overall business to excel. I want to be acknowledged for my results and have more global recognition and influence. In three years, I want to be promoted. My previous job, in Russia, was a turnaround situation. My work in the Middle East was also a turnaround situation, and so is the Asia department I am working in now."

Peter paused, and then out of the blue he said, "By the way, Lauren, the previous leader of this department was John's friend Patrick. When he was finally fired, I got his job."

Lauren believed she understood the message contained in Peter's words: "See, I got this job despite the fact that Patrick was a Tempus boy. I had the better connections." But before she chalked his words up to shameless bragging, she made sure to verify her assumption.

"That is quite an achievement, Peter. How did you get the job?" she asked.

"By having a good network to Tempus's top executives. I had better connections than Patrick," said Peter.

"I guess he wants me to know he has more gravitas than even Patrick," Lauren thought to herself. "He wants to make clear that he succeeded in getting his current position, and he might very well succeed in using his political acumen and his good results to reach the next level of management."

"I left my last job, in the Middle East, because it wasn't challenging enough. I was dealing with a group of incompetent people, and I got bored. I had a contact on the board at Tempus—I'd kept in touch with him while I was managing director of a small watch company. I reached out to him, and he gave me Patrick's job," alleged Peter.

"What do you like about your job here?" asked Lauren.

"I enjoy taking charge of the strategic reorganization of a department. I can talk to a lot of customers and make deals. I am good at turning around situations. However, I don't want to stagnate in this role. I want to be the global head of the fine-watch-making division. John is currently responsible for fine watches across the globe, but he might retire in a few years, and I intend to move into his position."

"So Peter is targeting John's job," thought Lauren. "Well, he doesn't lack ambition."

Peter then broke in animatedly, "I am almost scared of my own capabilities and ambition. At times, I want to be in my comfort zone to increase my confidence that I can achieve the results I want. But what John is doing is not rocket science. Nope, it is not rocket science," Peter repeated to himself.

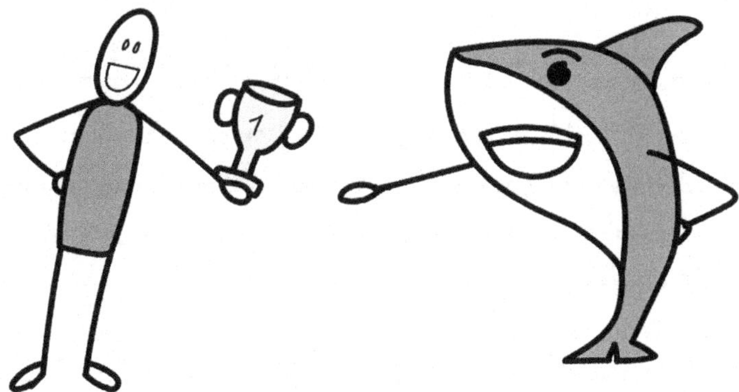

"When you retire, what would give you the most satisfaction if you were to look back?" ventured Lauren.

"Maybe when I retire, I will go back to academia. I like to do research work and bring together creative lines of thinking. In college, I was cum laude and teaching assistant to the dean of finance. When I taught, I liked giving something back to the master's students. It is interesting to observe students' approach to business. What I liked was the discussion and exploring different ideas with students from all over the world. I coached a protégé in Russia to take over a profitable company. He made a lot of money and later bought another company. I don't think he could have done it without me. Of course, I make more money than him, but he has done a pretty good job," continued Peter.

Lauren wondered how Peter would react if his protégé were outearning him. Would he become more competitive? "So money is a barometer of success for Peter," she thought to herself. "This is not unusual. And Peter likes to work in academia? That *is* a surprise. It sounds like he values knowledge and being recognized for his intellect and his learning, but he also seems to like the dialogue with his students. We need to explore this further at some point," she mused.

"What are your current frustrations or challenges, Peter?" asked Lauren. She could see he was relaxing and gaining confidence, and she was ready to investigate further. She could literally see Peter's mood shift and his body relax. He was more engaged in the process. Indeed, Peter was now beginning to confide in her.

The client's mood and body language will tell you when he or she is relaxed and confident enough to begin the real work of coaching. Don't rush.

"I work day and night for this company," Peter said. "I achieve outstanding results, and John comes to me to say I am 'a little tough' with my direct reports. What does he expect? I get outstanding results, and with subpar employees!"

On that note, he switched gears abruptly. "Talking about subpar, who is this Amanda you sent to talk to me?" Peter said angrily. His body tensed up again as he stood up from his desk and approached Lauren, towering over her.

"Peter, when you come up to me in anger, I get very uncomfortable. I feel as if you are going to attack me. Could you sit down again?" said Lauren, with more strength in her voice than she had used so far in her meeting with Peter. Peter kept looking at her but seemed surprised by her remark.

"I just wanted to make myself clear," he answered, but more softly this time, and he walked back to sit down at his desk again. Lauren's way of calmly standing her ground and sharing her feelings on the spot had taken the wind out of his sails. "I don't want to see her face again. Is that clear?"

"She is Tempus's new internal coach. She has some learning to do. Who is learning in your department, Peter?" asked Lauren, deftly shifting the conversation away from Amanda and back to the issues she wanted to discuss.

"My team members are all highly productive and experienced. I don't have time to teach them. HR's learning center should do that," he snapped.

"Peter, would you be comfortable working with me to get to the bottom of the issue with regard to your perceived leadership and how it might or might not be conducive to your longer term objectives? I think I can better support your success by gathering stakeholders' perceptions and getting back to you with the information. Then you can decide to move forward with the coaching or not," said Lauren.

"Can I integrate Tempus's board members into the survey as well as my boss, some of my peers, and my direct reports?" asked Peter.

"Sure," answered Lauren, knowing full well that Peter was intrigued to hear board members' perceptions of him. He was probably anticipating their praise and compliments. "How many participants would that entail, Peter?" she asked.

"Fourteen, but I could probably reduce my selection to twelve," answered Peter, looking at her to gauge her reaction. That meant she would be conducting fourteen interviews, because she would have to add two anonymous interviewees to Peter's twelve selected stakeholders. In all, that would mean two more respondents than was probably strictly necessary. Peter was always going to try to get more out of the deal-making, she assumed.

"Deal," Lauren heard herself answer.

"Well, then let's get started now," answered Peter. "What are the next steps?"

Chapter Review Questions

1. What are the important ingredients to convince Peter to be coached?
2. What steps of the leadership development process are covered in this chapter?
3. What is an action research methodology?
4. What are the steps to creating a Coworker Action Research Report?

CHAPTER 11

THE INITIAL TRIAD MEETING

A Balancing Act

———————————

Lauren's calendar was clear for the rest of the day, and she wanted to take advantage of the momentum built up by her conversation with Peter. If she waited and gave him time to think about it, he might start feeling defensive and refuse to participate in the Coworker Action Research Report. So she was happy to comply with Peter's suggestion that they start the process immediately.

PREPARING FOR THE COWORKER ACTION RESEARCH REPORTS

"The next step is to draw up your list of stakeholders, Peter," she told him.

Peter took a sheet of embossed, monogrammed letterhead from one of his drawers and started busily writing names. "Done," he said after a moment.

Step 1 of the Coworker Action Research Report: Have the client make a list of respondents for the research, then add participants recommended by HR or the client's boss.

"What next, Lauren?"

"Now we move to compiling the Coworker Action Research Report. First, you'll need to send an email to your stakeholders to let them know that you are doing a leadership development program. If the information comes from you, it demonstrates you are leading the process. Indicate that you will need their feedback to draw up an action plan."

Lauren rummaged through the papers she was carrying with her and picked out a form letter that her former employer, MKB Excellent Executive Coaching, used when beginning a coaching process.[i]

"Here's a template," she said, handing it over to him. "You can adapt this to your style."

---

i   For more information about MKB Excellent Executive Coaching, my coaching firm, see www.ExcellentExecutiveCoaching.com.

Letter to Stakeholders Participating in the Coworker Action Research Report

---

Dear —,

In view of my current and future leadership responsibilities, Tempus has offered me a leadership developmental program with a leadership coach. I found the proposal most interesting and accepted it. As part of the process, the coach will be conducting individual and confidential interviews with my boss, some of my peers, and my direct reports.

You have been selected to be one of the interviewees. During the interview, the coach will ask you two questions: (1) What are my leadership strengths? (2) What would make our working relationship even more productive?

The information from the interview will be strictly confidential. I will only receive a report with key themes: topics that at least two participants mentioned. No identifying information will be included. No specific details or examples will be given. My focus is on getting your insights, not learning who said what. Your feedback will be used to create my developmental action plan.

Lauren Schultz, PhD and Master Certified Coach (International Coach Federation), is a senior executive coach with extensive experience coaching leaders. She will look forward to spending thirty to forty-five minutes with you, face to face or by phone.

The face-to-face interviews will be held on June 15 and June 20. Please select a time <u>here.</u> Availability is on a first-come, first-served basis. If you cannot make these dates, please contact Lauren to schedule a call. She and I thank you in advance for your time. I appreciate your active participation in providing me with confidential feedback for my development.

Sincerely yours,

Peter Simmons

Step 2 of the Coworker Action Research Report: Have the client send a letter to stakeholders announcing that he or she is taking part in a leadership development program.

Peter read the letter, then looked at Lauren, "Okay, I can work with this," he said.

"Great," said Lauren. "In that case, the next step in the Coworker Action Research Report process is to set your long-term objectives. Once we have the completed report, we can see what you are doing or saying that is helping you toward your goal, and what might stop you from reaching it. And once you know your long-term objective, what do you want today from this leadership development coaching program?" she asked, surfing on his improved mood but aware that she should not have stacked two questions on top of each other.

Step 3 of the Coworker Action Research Report: Work with the client to set long-term objectives, so that once the report is debriefed, it will be clear what behaviors are helping or hindering the client from reaching his or her goals.

"I want to know how I am perceived as a leader. But mainly what I want is to reassure John and make sure he knows that I'm a skilled leader and I'm doing a great job with this division." Without waiting for Lauren to respond, Peter picked up the phone and snapped into the receiver, "Dorothé, come into my office!"

Almost before he had hung up the phone, his assistant, Dorothé, came running into the room. "Yes, Peter?" she asked timidly.

"Draft this email and send it to the people on this list. And I want it sent out right away, so don't take an hour to do it," he demanded harshly.

Dorothé nodded and left the room quickly with the paper in hand, although Lauren noticed that her jaw was clenched and her cheeks were flushed. She was anxious. Lauren was sympathetic—being Peter's assistant was sure to be a difficult job.

"What next?" Peter asked curtly, reading what Lauren had written on the whiteboard. "'Identify what you think are your biggest assets and drawbacks as a leader'. . . . I have answered that question," he said resolutely.

"What are your drawbacks, Peter?" Lauren inquired, wanting to know the gap between his perception of himself and the perceptions of his stakeholders. How self-aware Peter was would determine the approach Lauren would take when debriefing the Coworker Action Research Report.

"I get results above and beyond other leaders, which causes jealousy and discontent among my colleagues," stated Peter—somewhat arrogantly, Lauren thought.

"Anything else?" queried Lauren.

"No," he answered quickly.

Peter's brusque reply took Lauren by surprise. "Either Peter doesn't have enough confidence in our relationship to be open with me yet, or he is completely oblivious to how rude he can be," she thought. With all the upheaval taking place in his department, she had trouble believing he was completely unaware of his flaws.

But Peter had already moved on. "What next?" he said, thinking aloud. "The triad!" Impatiently and before Lauren could interrupt, he grabbed his phone and started dialing John. John's secretary must have answered that he was not in, because Peter hung up the receiver abruptly, without saying even goodbye.

Step 4 of the Coworker Action Research Report:
Determine how aware clients are of
their strengths and weaknesses.

"Wait, Peter," Lauren broke in. "Your immediate boss in the hierarchy is George. He needs to be part of this process. Why circumvent him and, by doing so, irritate him?"

"Because his opinion doesn't matter to me. He is envious of my results. I don't respect him, and I don't care what he says about me!" exclaimed Peter.

"Can George cause you trouble?" asked Lauren.

"No, he just spreads rumors and bad-mouths me, but I go directly to John to settle any problems," answered Peter.

"So, to avoid stirring up any problems, let's ask both John and George to attend the triad meeting and get to the root cause of the issue. Our objective is to find out their perception of the situation." Lauren paused and then said casually, so as not to get Peter's defenses up, "Don't interrupt them or justify yourself. What I mean is, do not try to clarify the facts. We are looking to understand how they perceive the situation. Let me obtain as much information as possible from the meeting. We want to find out exactly what their expectations are from the coaching and what behavioral changes they expect from you. We need key performance indicators, okay, Peter? Do you agree to let me lead the meeting?" probed Lauren.

"Okay, sure, let's get going," Peter answered. He was clearly irritated that the process was more involved and time consuming than he had expected, but he was also curious about the results.

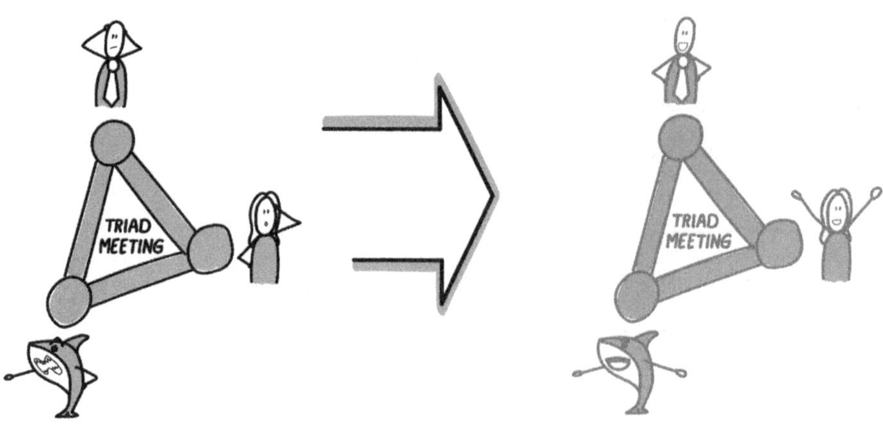

"Let me speak with John and George about the meeting and schedule a date with your secretary," said Lauren, straightening her skirt and heading out of Peter's office. The day had been full of ups and downs, beginning with her debriefing conversation with Amanda and then this challenging meeting with Peter, but Lauren was happy with how things had gone and felt a pleasant sense of accomplishment.

* * *

Several days later, just moments after Lauren had booked the initial triad meeting on everyone's calendar, her phone rang. She wasn't terribly surprised to find an anxious George on the line.

"Lauren, what is this meeting about?" he asked nervously.

"This is the first step in the coaching process with Peter," she told him. "The initial meeting will give you a chance to indicate what you expect from the Leadership Development Program. I will also ask you what Peter's strengths are and what would make your relationship with him more productive," Lauren told him, knowing full well that she needed to decrease his nervousness by telling him exactly how the meeting would pan out.

"I know we talked about this a few days ago in the canteen," Lauren continued, "but it will be helpful to have the conversation again with Peter present. I shall also ask John what the consequences will be if Peter does not change his ways and what will happen if he does improve. How does that sound?" continued Lauren.

"Great!" said George, sounding relieved. "But why is John going to be attending this meeting?"

"Peter asked for John to be present," she answered.

"Good," George sighed. "We will hear all the same messages at the same time."

Step 5 of the Coworker Action Research Report: Make sure the hierarchy is respected and the right key stakeholders are included in the triad meeting.

The Coach's Goals During the Initial Triad Meeting

1. Inform the meeting participants about the questions you will ask, and address any apprehension participants might have.

2. Lead the discussion by asking the following questions:
    - "What would be a good outcome of this coaching program?"
    - "What would you need to hear, feel, and see for the outcome to be good, bad, or excellent?"
    - "What is the first improvement step you would expect to see?"

3. Ask the boss what he or she will do to help the process (e.g., what event will the client and boss both attend, after which the client could receive immediate feedback about his or her leadership?).

4. Observe interactions between stakeholders and the client to compare perspectives later with the client during the coaching process.

5. Encourage the bosses to express what they might have said in private to the coach, the consequences if the leader does not change his or her behaviors, and the benefits of behavior change. Keep the conversation constructive, keep dialogue flowing, and make sure the core issues surface. Expectations should be expressed in very explicit, tangible, and specific terms.

6. Take notes on what is said during the meeting, for inclusion in the Coworker Action Research Report.

7. Reconfirm that the Coworker Action Research Report is for the

client's eyes only. Encourage the client to share with the boss areas he or she intends to work on and wants feedback on.

8. Explain the flow of the coaching process, and note that there will be another triad meeting after the coaching process is complete, to identify the changes in the client's leadership behavior.

THE TRIAD MEETING

The morning of the triad meeting was warm and sunny. Lauren arrived in the boardroom early, before any of the others, and stood at the window, taking in the view of Lake Geneva sparkling far below. The sky was so clear that she could glimpse Mont Blanc and the sailboats racing on the lake. How she would have liked to be on one of the boats instead of moderating what promised to be a thorny meeting among this triad.

"Why be nervous?" she asked herself. She had informed everyone attending the meeting about the questions she would ask and how she would lead the meeting. She had clearly said that the objective was for Peter's bosses to express their expectations and support for his leadership development and coaching program. She had warned Peter to listen to what was said and to control his emotions. She had addressed any apprehension the participants might have had, but she knew that George and Peter would have to control their frustration and that Peter, if exasperated, might explode.

Lauren knew John would be a good ally she could draw on to help calm the situation. He hated conflict and, like a mine detector, could defuse a potential explosive outburst before anyone could see it coming.

Her thoughts were interrupted when George walked into the boardroom, visibly nervous. He acknowledged Lauren with a nod and sat down toward the middle of the long wooden table, a few seats down from the head. Next Peter, tall and elegantly dressed, strutted in, looking sure of himself. He smiled. One could not help but notice his charisma and his powerful presence as he took his usual seat, to the right of John's chair at the head of the table. A few minutes later, John entered the room, greeted everyone warmly, and, with quiet confidence, sat down at the head of the table. Lauren, who had remained standing to greet everyone coming in, finally chose a seat to the left of John, directly across from Peter. As John turned to look at Lauren, she took the cue and started the meeting.

"Thank you all for coming," she said. "I know you all have busy schedules, so I'll jump right in. One goal for today's meeting is to set some objectives for Peter's leadership development program. John, what are the changes in leadership that you are expecting from Peter with this program?"

John turned to Peter, directing his response to him rather than Lauren. "Peter, you have done a lot for this company. I am personally indebted to you for turning around your department. You are a valued leader, and the company is investing in you with this leadership development program. But you need to abide by the leadership and management principles of the company. We cannot accept behaviors that infringe on the company's leadership principles."

"Could you be specific about exactly what behaviors you are referring to, John?" ventured Lauren.

During the triad meeting, encourage the bosses to be specific in their feedback rather than speaking in generalities. Ask them to clarify if necessary.

"Peter, you put enormous pressure on your direct reports to perform. Many valuable senior executives have left your department because they cannot stand the pressure. I understand that many of those who left might have been the weaker performers, but what I cannot accept is your lack of emotional control and empathy. Throwing a direct report's mobile phone across the room and breaking it into a thousand pieces does not exemplify Tempus's desired leadership behavior. You need to regain control of your emotions in all situations; otherwise, there will be serious consequences," John said with a frown. Lauren could tell he was not enjoying having to be so firm with Peter.

"Lack of emotional control?" Peter repeated, sounding stunned.

"I heard that the other day when you got angry with one of your direct reports, you grabbed his phone and threw it across the office, where it shattered in pieces. In our executive meeting last month, you lashed out at Robert so violently that he began to stutter and rushed out of the meeting. We cannot have this kind of behavior from our senior executives—or from anyone, for that matter," continued John.

Lauren glanced over to Peter and saw that he was ready to implode. She gave him a quick look to remind him not to react and to listen through to the end without interrupting, as they had mutually agreed. Peter had already given all his counterarguments to defend himself in prior meetings. It was time he listened, whether he agreed or not, to how John and George truly perceived him. Lauren saw her role as making sure John and George expressed their thoughts in a constructive way, but the harsh criticism was just too much for Peter.

"You wanted me to turn around the department," he told John angrily. "I did, and now you tell me I should have held employees' hands throughout the process? My job is to get results, not to be their babysitter," answered Peter, visibly perspiring with the effort to keep his voice controlled. His usual flamboyant charisma had seeped out of him. "You asked me to turn this division around," he repeated plaintively, clearly hurt that his mentor was scolding him.

John sensed that behind his apparent confidence, Peter was feeling betrayed and tried to placate him. "Peter, you have a phenomenal workload capacity," John said. "You have demonstrated great professionalism. You are devoted to the company's product and to the success of the business." John paused to let Peter absorb his strengths as a leader and regain control.

"You are used to working on your own in difficult markets," John continued. "You work well in crisis situations in emerging markets. You were hired to sort out this department, and you've done it. But you are too forceful when pushing issues through. Your interpersonal radar needs work. Granted, your brief for this position was to take charge and make it work, but your style is confrontational and aggressive, and that just does not work in an Asian market," continued John.

Lauren saw the subject veering back toward negative feedback and felt Peter had heard all he could take, so she quickly asked, "If Peter were doing an excellent job as a leader in a year's time, what would you expect to hear, feel, and see?"

When the balance of the triad meeting seems to be tipping too far toward negativity, subtly direct the line of questioning back to more constructive feedback.

"Peter would inspire," replied John. "There would be a positive change in the dynamics of teams working cross-functionally with him. People outside his team would want to work with him. He would delegate more. He would let go and trust others more. He lacks flexibility."

"What do you mean by lacking flexibility, John?" interjected Lauren. Generalities and vaguely defined terms would not be helpful to Peter; he needed clear and specific insights from those he respected if he were going to be convinced of the need for change.

"I mean his interpersonal radar needs to pick up cues when he is too forceful with people," replied John.

"Do you have any other success criteria, John?" solicited Lauren, subtly shifting the focus away from criticism and back to what John saw as markers for positive change.

"I'd consider Peter a success when everyone around him is positively involved and pleased to work with him," responded John.

"What support can you provide Peter during his leadership development program?" questioned Lauren. She wanted Peter to hear directly from John that John still thought highly of him and would be a willing and involved partner in this process.

"I am a firm supporter of Peter, and he can come to me any time to ask for feedback and advice," responded John, looking at Peter like a father who loved his son but was disappointed by his bad behavior.

"Any questions, Peter?" solicited Lauren.

"No," answered Peter, and he looked down at his pen, which he had been fiddling with throughout the meeting. Behind his seemingly confident composure was a contrite and hurt Peter, noted Lauren.

"What about you George?" questioned Lauren.

"Peter is smart, but he brings everything back to himself. I would be convinced that Peter's leadership behavior has changed when he is able to say, "Wow! The people and talent in this region amaze me. They are doing a phenomenal job.' When he does not alienate people or draw the glory to himself."

Peter shot George a look of disdain, angling his head away from John to hide the expression from his mentor. Lauren had a quick flashback of her four brothers quarreling for her father's attention. This endeared Lauren to both Peter and George, but she needed to be attentive not be drawn in emotionally. If she were going to help Peter, she had to remain as unbiased as possible and be a spectator and acute observer of the interplay. After all, her role was to be an objective researcher, but it was difficult when she felt their pain so acutely.

As she brought the triad meeting to a close, Lauren smiled to herself. On the whole, she was pleased with how the meeting had gone. John and George had shared enough concrete details to fuel the continuing coaching process, and Peter had responded fairly well. He would leave the meeting with a clear idea of what behavior was expected of him and what support he could expect from his bosses. He might not agree with them, but at least he had heard their concerns. Lauren could refer to and debrief these concerns later, during the coaching sessions.

The next step would be for Lauren and Peter to discuss their own perceptions of the situation. She would take Peter for a coffee after the triad meeting ended, so they could talk in a more relaxed environment. Then she would meet again with Amanda to move forward with the Coworker Research Action Report. Yes, Lauren thought to herself, the coaching process was going quite well . . . for the moment.

Chapter Review Questions

1. What information should be included in the letter to the participants of the Coworker Action Research Report?
2. What is the purpose of the triad meeting? What should be the coach's objectives?
3. What should the coach tell the participants to expect in the triad meeting? Why?
4. What behaviors should the coach encourage during the triad meeting? What should he or she discourage?

CHAPTER 12

GATHERING PERCEPTIONS

The Coworker Action Research Report

———

Later that day, Lauren stopped by Amanda's office to let her know how the triad meeting had gone. Although she knew Peter would never be willing to work with Amanda, Lauren still had high hopes that she could train Amanda in the Excellent Executive Coaching approach and watch her work successfully with other coaching clients. A few days earlier, when she had talked to Peter about this, to her surprise, he agreed to let Amanda collaborate on the Coworker Action Research Report, as long as she stayed behind the scenes.

Lauren found Amanda at her desk, going through some papers with deep concentration. She looked as crisp and professional as always in her stylish black suit, with a silk scarf at her neck. Amanda always seemed to dress with a special sense of French chic.

Hearing Lauren's light tap on her door, Amanda looked up. "How was your meeting with Peter?" she asked anxiously.

"I think it was very difficult for him. He was crushed to learn that John had lost confidence in him despite his outstanding financial results. He felt his hard work was being ignored. He kept telling me that his efforts were to no avail. He was dejected.

"After I emphasized the positive things John had said, Peter calmed down enough so that I could focus on what John wanted him to change. Right now, speaking to Peter about how to become more emotionally intelligent is like describing a helicopter to a blind man. He still doesn't have the framework to understand it. To develop rapport and to get to know Peter better, I eventually asked him about his background, but only when he started to calm down."

With Peter's permission, Lauren now shared the story with Amanda. Peter was the youngest child in a middle-class immigrant family who struggled to make ends meet. His oldest brother was mentally handicapped, and the family struggled to care for him. Peter's father was a professional ski coach, and his two other brothers, Christopher and James, were talented skiers, especially Christopher. Their father drove them hard, training them to be successful athletes. Peter was unlike his brothers, uncoordinated and awkward. He never really fit in.

When Peter was sixteen, Christopher was running late for ski practice after a heated discussion with his father. Driving too fast up the narrow mountain road, he went into a skid on a sharp, icy turn. His brakes locked, and the car broke through the guardrail and tumbled down the mountain. Christopher died in the accident.

James blamed his father for Christopher's death. He refused to put his skis on ever again and left home to grow organic food in the countryside.

Peter was devastated, but after his brother's death, he started to excel at school. His brothers had left a huge void in the family, and Peter gradually took over that space in the sunshine. He finished school first in his class and graduated cum laude from Harvard University.

"He has been a success story ever since," Lauren concluded. "This appears to be his biggest setback in years." She paused and looked at Amanda, who was wide-eyed as she took in the story.

"So what is next, Lauren?" she asked. "A 360-Degree Feedback Report?"

THE COWORKER ACTION RESEARCH REPORT VERSUS THE 360-DEGREE FEEDBACK REPORT

In human resources and industrial psychology, *360-degree feedback,* also known as multirater feedback, multisource feedback, or multisource assessment, is feedback from an employee's immediate circle. Most often, it includes direct feedback from an employee's subordinates, peers (colleagues), and supervisors, as well as a self-evaluation. It can also include feedback from external sources, such as customers, suppliers, or other interested stakeholders. The 360-Degree Feedback Report is one of the primary tools of the trade for coaches and human resources managers.

"No," answered Lauren quickly. "I suggest a customized Coworker Action Research Report. This is what we always used at MKB Excellent Executive Coaching. The 360-Degree Feedback Report isn't specific enough to be useful in this case."

"Why?" interrupted Amanda.

"The feedback is too general to give a clear indication of the specific behaviors that are posing a problem. From the report, we need to be able to separate Peter's good leadership behavior from his abrasive ways," said Lauren.

"Let me give you a few examples," she continued. "Questions on the 360-Degree Feedback Report are predetermined and answered on a response scale from 1 (the lowest) to 5 (the highest). So let's say Peter is evaluated as a 1 for communication. Now he knows that he communicates badly, but he doesn't know what that means. Docs he stutter? Does he not walk the floors to say hello to his team members? Does he not cascade the company's strategy clearly enough to others, or does he speak to them condescendingly? 'He does not communicate well' is too nebulous a comment."

Amanda nodded in comprehension. "That makes sense."

"In Peter's case you might assume that the respondents meant he talks to people condescendingly. However, even if your assumption is correct, the respondents might have meant that he screams and bangs on his desk when he is angry or he always reads his emails when direct reports are standing in his office trying to talk to him. In both these cases, Peter is condescending. We need specific, detailed examples, which the 360-Degree Feedback Report just does not give. When we interview respondents instead, we can probe them until we learn about specific, verifiable behaviors.[i] Specific information can more readily be translated into an action plan," asserted Lauren.

---

i   These insights are drawn from my conversations with Dr. Laura Crawshaw.

Amanda didn't seem convinced. She turned to a 360-Degree Feedback Report lying open on her desk and flipped to the last page. "But Lauren," she said, "look here, there's a space for the respondent to leave comments. Specific examples could be given there." Amanda looked both confused and annoyed; her eyebrows were knitted together on her pretty face.

"These qualitative remarks and comments are insufficient and even dangerous, for two essential reasons," explained Lauren. "First, they are written in the respondent's own style, so it's easy to figure out who wrote them. In a multicultural corporate environment like Tempus, where people speak different languages, it is even easier to decipher who said what by the manner and the language they express themselves in."

"Then respondents can all decide to write up their comments in English," exclaimed Amanda.

"Wouldn't you be able to distinguish a native English speaker's response from a foreigner's?" asked Lauren.

"Yes, okay, you have made your point," grumbled Amanda.

"If Peter identifies who made any negative comments, he will surely respond aggressively, and anonymity is compromised. So the 360-Degree Feedback Report is not the best choice for maintaining privacy," stated Lauren.

"Okay," said Amanda. "What can we do instead?"

"MKB Excellent Executive Coaching uses the Coworker Action Research Report. It's a qualitative and inductive interview process that makes fewer assumptions and hypotheses at the initial stages of the research. The researcher is not sure about the type and nature of the research findings and themes until the study is completed. Each Coworker Action Research Report has different findings according to the issue at hand, and, therefore, the process is inductive—something like 'customization,' in business jargon. No two reports are the same, and we need to be open-minded to what we may discover," explained Lauren.

The Excellent Executive Coaching Process's Coworker Action Research Reports are far more effective than 360-degree feedback. They are based on inductive reasoning, begin with no assumptions, and yield reliable data—all while guarding respondents' anonymity.

ELEMENTS OF THE COWORKER ACTION RESEARCH REPORT

"In inductive reasoning," Lauren continued, "we begin with specific observations, then start to detect patterns and categories and formulate some tentative hypotheses that we can explore. We end by developing some general conclusions or theories. Peter's report will include observations of him and his patterns of behavior. The coach continues to conduct interviews until the same specific feedback is gathered from several respondents and is repetitive." Lauren paused, wondering whether this was getting too technical for Amanda, who was new to research.

"Why are the interviews not over until the same specific data are gathered by several respondents?" queried Amanda.

"Because the data gathered need to be reliable. If several people have witnessed the same behavior, the information is assumed to be accurate and consistent. In Peter's case, you want to avoid integrating comments from a person who has a personal vendetta against him and might make up stories. So at least two respondents need to provide similar feedback or observations before you can consider the feedback valid. In a 360-Degree Feedback Report, lies from Peter's enemies would skew the averages."

"That makes sense," Amanda nodded.

"Another important element for the success of this process is that Peter will be the only one to receive this report. We will be going around the company getting feedback from his stakeholders on his leadership. This will likely be an unsettling process for Peter. He will be less apprehensive about losing face or about the report being used against him if he is the only one to receive it. He will also be the one to decide what changes to make. This will give him back some control, trust, and comfort with the coaching process."

Lauren continued, "Once he receives the Coworker Action Research Report, Peter and I will become co-researchers to explore why stakeholders responded the way they did and what behavior strategies he can enact to alter those negative perceptions that are limiting his career and dampening his long-term goals within Tempus. Of course, these changes will correspondingly reduce the pain victims are experiencing from his emotional outbursts." Lauren paused to pour a hot cup of coffee for each of them from the carafe on Amanda's desk.

"Our role as coaches is to develop Peter's self-awareness and, by doing so, his interpersonal acumen—that is, his emotional intelligence. Greater EQ will provide Peter with different ways to react to a situation that frustrates or stresses him. He might be so focused on results that he is blinded to relationships."

In the Excellent Executive Coaching Process,
the coach and client work as a team to develop
the client's self-awareness and EQ.

Amanda gratefully accepted the mug of coffee Lauren handed her and said, "Isn't it *obvious* that Peter should stop screaming and banging on the table? Why can't we simply tell him to stop it? It is causing him to be perceived as a brute. How can Peter be so brilliant in business and so blind about how people see him?" she asked, perplexed.

"Amanda, I have seen many bright leaders receive 360-Degree Feedback Reports for five consecutive years but still not know how to change negative perceptions that are ruining their career. They need more help and guidance," Lauren sighed.

"Won't these interviews further demonize Peter within the company? Won't they just emphasize the flaws in Peter's leadership?" interrupted Amanda.

"The letter we send to participants indicates that Peter is undertaking a leadership development process. This is a neutral statement, but you're right that many people will assume the process includes remedial coaching. The benefit is that the letter sends an indirect message that the company will address misbehavior and uphold its leadership principles."

"I see," said Amanda. "So ideally the interviews might help change the corporate culture, too."

"That's right," Lauren agreed. "To avoid demonizing the client, I like to finish an interview by asking, 'What would make your relationship more productive?' instead of inquiring about the client's weaknesses. This question implies a relationship between the client and the respondent and stresses that *both* are accountable for making the relationship more productive."

Lauren continued, "As I mentioned, getting the stakeholders involved in Peter's behavioral change makes the process systemic and effective. Peter's initial attempts to improve his abrasive behavior might be awkward. If his direct reports don't realize he is undergoing a leadership development program, they might see his attempts to change as distressing, suspicious, and manipulative. They might think, 'Why is he trying to be nice to us? What is his agenda? What else does he want from us?' Their suspicion will push Peter back into his old behavior. He will feel that the process has failed despite his best efforts to change his ways.

"If his direct reports have participated in the feedback process and are aware that Peter is trying to improve, they will likely be much more lenient and encouraging about his initial awkward attempts to change. Forewarning employees that they are also an integral part of Peter's behavioral change process will likely change their perception. Stakeholders will be expecting changes and looking for them," asserted Lauren.

"Well, change should be easy enough. Peter's misbehavior is obvious!" emphasized Amanda.

"Maybe. But keep in mind that before Peter can change any behavior, he needs to know what triggers his reactions. He might say that he loses his temper because his direct reports are not proactive, or that he feels that they are disrespectful of his authority. What assumptions and threats does he perceive that are provoking his behavior? His *behavior* is the tip of the iceberg. We need to explore his *belief system*. We are not psychotherapists, so we won't delve into his past or his unconscious to explain the cause of such behavior. We will simply explore his mind-set, his fears and hopes.

"After all, Peter is brilliant and driven. He has an IQ well above most people's. A poorly thought-out remark by a direct report might exasperate him, and it becomes extremely visible in his nonverbals or might provoke a violent, frustrated reaction. Do you think his direct reports are likely to propose new ideas after Peter has screamed at them for being stupid, for example?" asked Lauren.

Once clients are aware of their negative behavior,
work with them to discover the belief system, fears,
and assumptions the behavior is based on.

"They would certainly come better prepared next time. Maybe that is what Peter wants," interjected Amanda.

"Yes, the fear of being threatened with attacks from Peter will likely cause the direct report to be better prepared next time," Lauren agreed. "But we need to help Peter learn how to become a demanding leader instead of an abrasive leader. The demanding boss critiques the work, not the person, and tries to figure out what has impeded him or her from succeeding, then remove those barriers."

"This takes a lot of time to explain and train," protested Amanda.

"Yes, it does, but a leader like Peter cannot do everything himself. He needs to work with and through people to reach the full potential of his leadership."

"Okay," Amanda conceded. "So what's the next step, then?"

"Once Peter has identified his belief system, he will need to test out new, more productive behaviors. Peter has choices in the way he may react to a frustrating situation. We need to highlight those choices and expand his leadership repertoire," said Lauren.

"What do you mean by expanding Peter's leadership repertoire?" solicited Amanda.

"My assumption is that Peter reacts to frustrating situations in a similar way each time—that is, with different forms of aggression. Our job is not only to help Peter better manage his disruptive emotions and keep his impulses under control but also to give him a wider array of leadership styles according to the circumstances, so that he can better excel at reaching his goals while having a positive impact on Tempus's organizational climate.

"To have flexibility in their leadership styles, leaders need certain essential competencies. They need to have self-confidence, for example. They need to have empathy and be good at communicating and building relationships. So let us identify Peter's competencies and what he needs to work on."

"That sounds like a tall order," Amanda said wryly.

Effective leaders can access an array of leadership styles, according to the person and to circumstances.

"So now, Amanda, let us agree that you and I will be collecting data from the interviewees. Usually I like the interviews to be conducted by someone who has never met the respondents, so that his or her perceptions are as unbiased as possible by any prior information. But John wants you to learn more about the leadership development process. Amanda, I must confess I am not comfortable with both of us being internal to the organization. You need to sign this confidentiality agreement that anything you hear during these interviews, you will not share with anyone inside or outside Tempus. Do you agree?" asked Lauren.

"Yes, of course," answered Amanda, eager to be part of the research process.

"Here is the list of respondents Peter has selected and the ones HR has added for anonymity's sake," said Lauren, visibly pleased to leap into action. "I'd like to hold the interviews in the employee lounge. It's comfortable and intimate, which will help the interviewees feel as relaxed as possible. The door can be closed, so participants won't worry about being overheard."

COMPILING THE COWORKER ACTION RESEARCH REPORT

Lauren and Amanda spent the next several days interviewing the chosen respondents. After they had completed the first two interviews, they met to discuss what they had learned so far. To give Amanda some practice with the method, Lauren asked her to combine the raw data from both of them and build the Coworker Action Research Report. She summarized the report-building process for Amanda.

How to Compile the Coworker Action Research Report

1. Combine both interviewers' notes about the client's leadership behaviors.
2. Regroup similar observations by the different respondents into patterns or categories.
3. Take out any identifying material (e.g., lingo and specific examples).
4. Suggest specific action steps the client could implement to alter negative perceptions.
5. Identify coaching questions that could be addressed after the Coworker Action Research Report debriefing session.

"Lauren, why list a series of quick action steps?" Amanda asked. "Don't we want Peter to reflect more on his behaviors?"

"Peter might be disturbed after debriefing the report. He will have a strong urge to 'fix' the situation as quickly and effectively as possible. Let's leverage this positive energy of his and give him something easy to work on that will give him immediate results and quick wins."

Giving a client quick action steps during debriefing offers him or her a sense of control and forward motion.

Lauren continued explaining the process to Amanda. "To save time, you need not categorize the strengths into themes. Remember, an issue must be mentioned by at least two respondents to be included in the report—once the information is redundant, you know it can be a theme. Executives like their reports to be to the point. An executive summary will suffice. I shall address the more complex issues during the coaching process."

Lauren sighed, wishing Amanda could observe Peter's debriefing session, but Peter was adamant that he did not want to work with Amanda.

* * *

Over the next two weeks, Lauren was very busy conducting the stakeholder interviews for the Coworker Action Research Report. As she expected, the feedback about Peter varied widely from person to person: Some people praised his incredible drive and strong work ethic, while others focused more on his angry outbursts and his impatience with his direct reports.

Rather than compiling the report herself once the data were collected, Lauren asked Amanda to give it a try. Amanda was nervous and didn't feel she was quite ready, but Lauren reassured her that they would go over her work together before debriefing the report with Peter. Lauren was enjoying the opportunity to act as a mentor for Amanda, and she looked forward to seeing Amanda's first attempt at the Coworker Action Research Report.

Chapter Review Questions

1. What are the risks and limitations of the 360-Degree Feedback Report?
2. What is action research?
3. What is the process for conducting the Coworker Action Research Report interviews?
4. What steps should the coach take to protect the anonymity of the interviewees?

CHAPTER 13

FINDING PATTERNS IN THE FEEDBACK

How the Coworker Action Research Report Works

Two weeks later, Lauren was in her office when Amanda stopped in. "Here is the Coworker Action Research Report for Peter," she said. "I gave it my best shot. I was nervous writing it up. I struggled with making the comments anonymous enough," said Amanda softly as she handed the report to Lauren.

Lauren skimmed through the document, nodding with approval. "This is good work, Amanda," she praised. "You've done a very nice job. Have a seat, and let's go through the report together."

After giving some positive feedback, Lauren pointed to a line on the first page of the report. "Look at this English idiom—it could easily be attributed to someone who tends to use that phrase. You had better change the sentence to convey its meaning and use neutral language." She marked the spot in pencil so Amanda could go back and change it later.

"Oops!" Lauren said. "Here are several specific examples that you must take out of the report. Specific examples help us understand the contributor's meaning, but they should be summarized or even deleted in the final report. Also, sentences in the third person are more neutral. These brief sentences might warrant some explaining during the debriefing session, but at least we make a thorough effort to protect respondents' anonymity."

They went through the rest of the report, with Lauren pointing out places where small adjustments were needed. "You did a good job of grouping observations and categorizing them into themes from the interview notes, Amanda," said Lauren encouragingly.

"Thank you," said Amanda. "I worked hard on it."

In a Coworker Action Research Report, use generic, neutral language, and avoid giving specific examples. This helps preserve contributors' anonymity.

When they had finished, Lauren said, "Okay, Amanda, let's meet tomorrow afternoon after you have made those alterations. From this exercise, I'll teach you how to create a truthful report while protecting the participants' anonymity. We'll also create a possible action plan to discuss with Peter."

ORGANIZING THE FEEDBACK INTO THEMES

The next afternoon, when Amanda entered Lauren's office with the revised report, she seemed a little more confident. She handed her work to Lauren, and they read through the document together.

The Coworker Action Research Report

Question 1: What Are the Leader's Strengths?

Theme 1: He is well-respected and professional with clients.

1. Peter has an *outstanding workload capacity* and *works extremely hard* toward clear objectives. He is passionate and responsible. He attends to detail and *wants to know everything*.
2. He is devoted to products, to clients, and to the success of the business.
3. He has high expectations of himself and others, even people who don't report directly to him.
4. He is very *knowledgeable* about what is happening globally. He knows what success looks like. He has a broad and *in-depth knowledge* of the company's background.
5. He thinks *strategically* and can immediately point out when someone has made a mistake in their strategic thinking. He has both a *big-picture view* and a detailed view of the situation. He is clear, globally oriented, strategic, and direct.
6. He is an outstanding *troubleshooter* and can solve any issue. He inspires me.
7. He is *straightforward*, direct, even honest. He is not afraid to share his feedback or opinion. He is candid and easily decipherable. Peter knows what he wants. He explains where he is coming from.
8. He *demands excellence.*

9. He has *good ideas* about what needs to change and happen. He looks at events and has a unique approach. He thinks about the global implications.

10. Intellectually, he is a *sharp thinker* and has the necessary credentials. He thinks quickly. Peter is *quick, decisive*, and articulate and has a clear vision. He is *dynamic and fast moving*. He is very *smart*. He is *articulate* about what has been done in the company, about the customer's needs, and about what needs to be done.

"Amanda, these comments might have come from Peter's defenders and the people in his in-group. It would be good to explore what allowed Peter to develop confidence in them," mused Lauren.

---

11. He has a fair amount of confidence.

12. He has an *elephant's memory*, and he *reads a lot*. Peter can pick any subject and say what has already been done, what worked, and what did not work. He knows what is happening around the globe.

13. Peter is used to *working on his own* and in difficult markets and is used to crisis situations in emerging markets. He was hired to sort out difficult situations. Our China division has a five-year history of being badly managed, and, in all fairness, his contract for this position was to be in charge and *make this region thrive*.

Question 2: What Would Make the Relationship More Productive?

1. He is smart and knowledgeable, and it is surprising that there is a side to him that will follow instructions strictly if they come from John, even if the instructions don't make sense to Peter. He seems secure and confident, and it amazes me that he is so *influenced by John*. In terms of teamwork, it is depressing and confusing that he is so abrasive with us and submissive with John.

2. He dominates group meetings and does not listen to team members. He comes with ready-made solutions and does not consult the experts.

3. He likes to work independently and seems to have an agenda because *he drives John's campaign* as if he were on a mission. He is so dependent on whatever John thinks of him. He insists on pushing the party line rather than being accepting of possible alternatives from others.

4. He can be *too strategic* and miss out on the local opportunities. He is focused on driving the corporate agenda. He cares about what the boss and the global team think of him but less of the local market and what opportunities it offers. It does not look like he is in the trenches with his local teams.

FORMULATING QUICK ACTION STEPS

"So, Amanda, if you had the opportunity to coach Peter, how would you proceed? What quick action steps could Peter take, given the above comments?" queried Lauren.

"Hmm. When in meetings, he could reformulate what his direct reports said, and if their idea conflicts with the corporate agenda, instead of dismissing it out of hand, he could ask them how their plan can be realigned with the corporate strategy. Or he could take some time to think about it before deciding. People might feel better if they knew he was taking their ideas into consideration. Am I right?" asked Amanda, nervous she might be on the wrong track.

"Yes, good job," said Lauren encouragingly. "This could be a quick action step, and you could even make a coaching exercise of reformulating what people say before he answers. At first, repeating in his words what people say to him will feel very unnatural to him. However, this technique will encourage him to listen what the other person is saying before he answers, and it will also tell the other person that he has listened."

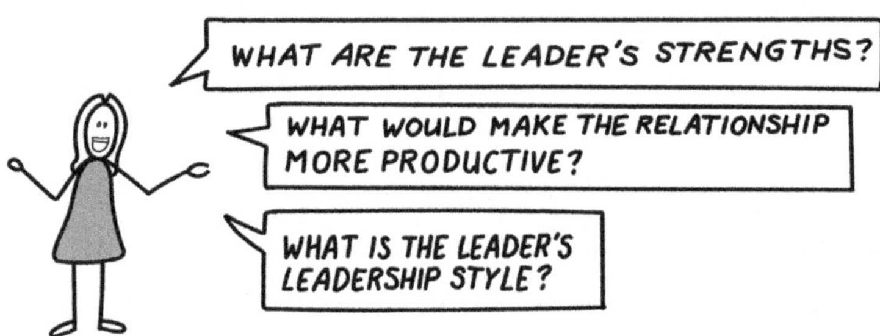

"Won't it feel artificial?" Amanda asked. "Won't the person speaking feel that Peter is making fun of them or imitating them?"

"Surprisingly, if it's well done, people feel listened to and understood. However, if it is done too repetitively and in the exact words of the person speaking, the speaker and the listener can both feel it is unnatural. This is why Peter needs to practice this behavior change during the coaching sessions."

"That makes sense," said Amanda. "What do you think of the revised report?"

"First of all, you are doing too much of the work for Peter. Your work is to ask simple questions to get him thinking and ultimately have an 'insight' moment. Remember, it is not your job to know the answers. You just need to ask questions so that he starts exploring and developing answers. During the coaching process, you could also ask open-ended questions like, 'Why do you think you are perceived as subservient to the CEO? What does John represent to you? What might make people think you perceive your boss, George, as stopping you from doing business?'"

Theme 2: Peter lacks sensitivity to others, does not listen, and does not participate in team activities.

5. He *lacks sensitivity*. He is tactless in the way he says things. His interpersonal radar is broken, and he does not easily receive cues.

6. He is dedicated and has his own views. The flip side of this is that he can be *stubborn* and at times can't see things from others' point of view.

7. He has little sensitivity to what is required by others. He does not know how to pitch himself to engage people outside of his in-group. He has little to no empathy or social radar.

8. Peter needs to learn to connect and to *package messages* so that others can hear them.

9. He is not tactful. He will *criticize direct reports* on their personal attributes *in front of other direct reports.*

10. He *does not give an explanation* when he rejects a coworker's idea. He can be curt and condescending. He seems to be saying, "My ideas are too complicated to explain to you, so just believe me and get on with it."

"Okay, Amanda, given these comments, what quick action steps would you suggest for Peter?" Lauren asked.

Amanda thought for a moment. "Well," she said, "I would tell him not to do the work or write up reports for his employees. He should try to direct them but let them integrate their thoughts and ideas into what they present. He should compliment them when he thinks they have completed a specific task well. He should analyze whether the direct report is unwilling or unable, and respond accordingly. Oh, and if he rejects an employee's idea, then he should explain why, and name some elements of the idea that he found interesting. How am I doing? Did I miss anything?"

Lauren thought for a moment, then commented, "'Stop criticizing direct reports in front of others' is a good quick action step. It is a terrible thing to do to people. You could ask him how he thinks it makes them feel. Has he ever been criticized in front of others? What was his experience, his feeling? How did he feel when John made comments about his leadership at the triad meeting?

"Even if he says, 'It doesn't bother me,' ask him if, from this feedback, he thinks it bothers others. The key is to develop his empathy by putting him in other people's shoes to see how they perceive him, how this perception affects how they feel about him, and perhaps also how it interferes with his management ability," suggested Lauren before reading on.

Question 3: *What Is Peter's Leadership Style?*

Theme 1: Peter is aggressive.

1. Some people *do not want to work with him* and only agree to deal with him through emails.
2. He likes to *force the issue through*.
3. Peter *attacks verbally and personally* with questions like, "How can you not know what is going on?"
4. Some people are *afraid to talk to him* and *unwilling to work with him*. People are not sure whether they are going to be attacked.
5. When he encounters resistance, he becomes *aggressive, hierarchical,* very top-down. He does not collaborate.

Theme 2: Peter is a perfectionist.

6. He cannot do something less than 100 percent. He practically completes projects before he hands them over to his direct reports, which gives little space for others to work things out themselves.

Theme 3: Peter is competitive.

7. He competes with me in my field. He *practices one-upsmanship*.
8. The problem is his attitude. He *makes others look weak*, especially the client. It is not intentional. He might say something like, "How can you not know what is going on?" It's one-upsmanship.

"Well," Amanda interjected, "here I would suggest as a quick action step: 'Always acknowledge the expertise of the other.' You are experienced in this area, Lauren, so how might you address this issue? What do you think?"

"This is an opportunity to create insight," Lauren said. "A coach might ask Peter, 'Why do you think people perceive you as trying to make them look weak? How do you think it makes them feel? Has anyone ever tried to make you look weak? Why do you accuse them of not knowing what's going on?'"

Theme 4: Peter is pushy.

9. Peter should be more pull and less push and should *take the back seat more often.*
10. Peter is *pushy and pressures people.* This leads to people turning in subpar work just to drive him away. When they need more time and they feel Peter's request is unreasonable, they scan what has already been done and send it to him.

Amanda lifted her eyes from the report to Lauren and said, "The quick action step I wrote here is, 'Give them clear deadlines and tell them when you are going to come back and ask them for something.'"

Lauren answered, "Another way of communicating it could be, 'You have a great reputation as a man who gets things done, so it's appropriate to verify that your employees are meeting the deadlines you set. Tell them when you expect the work to be done, then don't pressure them about it in the meantime. If you cannot resist checking in, offer them your help by asking how the project is coming along and whether you can do anything to support the person.' This is a good one and simple to carry out," said Lauren, smiling.

---

11. When he does not get an answer, he *pressures people.*
12. A couple of days after our opinions clash, he will renegotiate. He is pushy when he is frustrated and his point is not taken. He has a strong personality and style, and he should not change that, but he

should play it differently. He needs to let go earlier. It is important to Peter to *win the argument* even if he is aware of the cost to the relationship. He hopes to make it up later.

Amanda said, "A quick action step I wrote is, 'Choose which arguments are essential and critical to win in the moment.'"

Lauren replied, "Good. And a coaching question could be to ask how Peter could use more of a lobbying strategy."

---

13. I was warned before taking my job that he is *pushy and dominating* and that he takes credit and points fingers when things go wrong.

14. Peter *finger-points* instead of being objective. He should search for a solution and ask what happened before accusing someone. His approach and tone should be more solution oriented instead of accusatory.

"What was your quick action step here, Amanda?" asked Lauren.

"'Find ways to compliment direct reports or other professionals in meetings, but only if you believe what you're saying. When there is a problem, take more time to find out what happened,'" Amanda answered, then added, "This is common sense."

"To go deeper, Amanda, ask, 'What were the causes that brought on the problem? What could we do to not have this happen again?' Note that I said *we*, Amanda. Remember, we want to make it clear that we are Peter's partners in change and are co-researchers."

---

15. He gives more than 100 percent to his work. Work is his life. He should start having a life. He doesn't inspire people to work like him. He is *not relaxed*.

"In this case," Amanda stated, "I would remind Peter to continue to work as much as he wants but to remember that not everyone will perceive that as positive."

"Good point," Lauren agreed. "Now turn it into a question, such as, 'How do stakeholders perceive the long work hours you put in?' And keep asking the same question about different stakeholders until you get Peter to start seeing from different people's perspectives and gain more insight into his deeper motivation for working so hard."

Theme 5: Peter takes the credit for successes.

16. People should be positively involved. He *alienates people* and *draws the glory to himself*. He does not always get people to follow through.
17. He *steals the show*. He pushes people away. Others need praise and acknowledgement, too.

"Okay, I get it," said Amanda excitedly. "My quick action step—'A key motivator is positive feedback. Use more of it'—should become a coaching question that leads Peter to explore what motivates different stakeholders." Amanda grinned, beginning to understand the process.

"A quick action step can be to the point," Lauren agreed, "but it is better if it comes from Peter. Peter is action-oriented, like a lot of executives, so he will appreciate going immediately into action after the probable shock of seeing himself as incompetent interpersonally. However, the ensuing coaching process is the opportunity to dive deeper into the underlying issues that drive his behavior in the first place."

Lauren paused to eat a piece of the Swiss chocolate she always kept on her desk, offering some to Amanda. "You might start a conversation with Peter by saying, 'You are the boss and are an outstanding professional, and like a parent, you need to encourage the juniors when they take their first steps. As we can see from the feedback, they see you as an exceptional professional and compliment you for being sincere.' This will go a very long way."

---

18. His work is important to him. He *wants to be successful* and be recognized. He takes the credit and makes us understand that the work was his idea.

Amanda looked at Lauren, "What coaching question would you start with here?"

"Well, a possible conversation opener could be, 'You are the parent and boss now, and your role is to motivate your team to excel. You are already excellent at your job. Reassure yourself that you are extremely competent. I certainly perceive you that way. Maybe no one did that for you in the past. This might make it hard for you to do it for others. But today, you are so senior that a key component of your job must be to encourage your team,'" answered Lauren.

"I like that," said Amanda, smiling but still insecure about whether she could handle a debriefing with a brilliant and abrasive jerk.

Theme 6: Peter's body language is informative.

19. He wears his mood on his sleeve. When he walked into the HR department, he looked like he was going to attack. He *emits hostility* and looks like he is going to snap.

"Be very careful not to mention which department he walked into, as it might identify the person," interjected Lauren.

---

20. *Quick-tempered* and *impatient*. When he is angry, you can tell by his body language. He points his finger at the person. He does

not listen. He *takes the power.* He makes you feel stupid that the information is obvious and you should have known. He turns his head away and walks off.

21. He is frowning and in a *bad mood* most of the time. He only smiles with clients.

22. Peter has a *difficult personality.* When he gets mad, he walks away annoyed, rolls his eyes, and gives a condescending and cynical smile.

Theme 7: Peter is stubborn.

23. He is convinced that his answers are the best, and he is blind to other options. He has strong opinions and is *convinced he has the absolute truth.* He pushes others' opinions away. For example, he will say, "I have already thought of that and it will not work."

Theme 8: Peter has difficulty with delegating.

24. He does not set clear expectations.

25. His messages do not always trickle down. People are *not fully informed* about what he wants.

26. When people are not clear on what Peter wants from them, they go to others and ask them to make a decision.

27. At times, Peter *does not clearly enumerate priorities* or schedule timelines. He implies that the work needs to be done immediately. Junior people don't go back to Peter to clarify the timeline. He should explain the rules. Besides this, he is *very organized.* He is in control and has thought the process through.

28. What we discussed was not always reflected in the project presented to me. He was not always able to persuade his team to follow his orders.

Lauren, observing that Amanda was beginning to feel overwhelmed, accelerated her explanation by pretending to be in the room with Peter. "Peter, you are traveling a lot, which makes it all the more challenging to direct three teams in different regions. This being said, you need to give directions in baby steps for the more junior staff. How can you do that?"

Lauren pulled open her desk drawer and brought out a file folder. "Amanda, always have articles handy that you could share with your client on a specific topic that you have discussed during the coaching. What might be helpful here is Ken Blanchard's Situational Leadership Model or this article by Daniel Goleman, 'Leadership That Gets Results.'"[1]

Amanda enthusiastically interrupted, "I did not write an action step here, but what I could say is . . . hmmm. 'It sounds like what you present to the client and agree on is not always reflected in what is later delivered. To show your clients you have listened to them, bring your notes from earlier discussions and address them when you deliver the product.' What do you think?" questioned Amanda.

"A good quick action step," Lauren said with a smile.

---

29. He is senior so we do what he says, and the results are his.

"Lauren, it's your turn," said Amanda mischievously, beginning to really enjoy the process.

Lauren didn't want to overload her protégé with more than she could absorb in one session, so she took advantage of Amanda's challenge to wrap up their meeting. "A quick action step would be to encourage Peter to change his 'the results are mine' approach to 'the results are ours' and to become a team player. As a boss, you get the blame, they get the credit. They will love him for it, and John might perceive Peter more as a leader defending his team. Peter might also want to talk with John about *how* he is developing his direct reports' competencies. This was a key objective John expressed during the triad meeting.

"This approach is more directive than exploratory, but it gets to the point. The best questions and remarks depend on the 'coaching moment.' We can prepare the coaching questions now as best we can, but during the coaching, we have to 'dance with the client.' How and when we question all depends on our relationship with the coaching client in the moment," commented Lauren, pleased that Amanda was so eager to learn.

Lauren quickly glanced through the remaining part of the report. There were a few more themes, but someone was knocking at her door with increasing persistence.

"Amanda, forgive me," said Lauren as she stood up from her desk and walked briskly to the door. She was just about to open it when someone burst into the room, nearly knocking her over.

"God, it takes forever for you to answer the door!" shouted Peter. As he looked past Lauren's shoulder, he glanced at Amanda and gave her a condescending smile, rolling his eyes in exasperation. "I need to see you now, Lauren!" he continued, but he tempered his tone a bit at the sight of Lauren's surprised face.

She calmly answered, "Peter, I am busy now. I'll meet you in your office in an hour."

Before she had even completed her sentence, Peter had stomped out of her office. Lauren sighed. Clearly there was a lot of work ahead of her.

Chapter Review Questions

1. Create more action steps from the report above.
2. In a role-play, practice debriefing with your colleague the above Coworker Action Research Report tactfully and with empathy for your coachee, then switch roles. Finally, debrief.
3. In a role-play, identify three qualities you have and three areas where you could use improvement. Have a colleague identify how to leverage the qualities and coidentify action steps to improve. Then debrief.

CHAPTER 14

DEBRIEFING THE COWORKER ACTION RESEARCH REPORT

The Coaching Starts

***

As Peter stormed out of her office, Lauren turned to Amanda, visibly unsettled by Peter's startling interruption. Reaching out to take Peter's Coworker Action Research Report from Amanda, she jotted down a few notes, then gave it back.

"Please get this report corrected immediately and bring it back to me," requested Lauren, who was clearly stressed under her apparently calm demeanor. Amanda was beginning to know Lauren's more subtle changes in behavior. Tucking the report under her arm, she rushed nervously out of the office without saying a word. She was keen to do a good job. Within fifty minutes, she was already back to hand over the corrected report.

"Lauren, what are you going to do next?" inquired Amanda eagerly.

Lauren had her coaching process in mind and had already written it down for Amanda on the whiteboard. As she walked Amanda through it, she said, "Keep in mind that even though I've written it out in a linear form on the whiteboard, the coaching process is iterative. Your intuition, combined with how best to leverage the interest and energy of your client, will determine the flow of the conversation. Globally, though, it is important to know where you are in the overall process all the time."

Lauren's Planned Coaching Process for Peter

- Ask Peter about his background. Identify his unmet needs by examining significant events in his early development. Identify his current and past aspirations and frustrations to better understand the system he lives in and what might have provoked him to start reacting defensively and abrasively.
- Identify whether a chronic pattern of abrasive behavior emerged from the Coworker Action Research Report.
- Debrief with Peter the patterns and themes that emerged from the Coworker Action Research Report.
- Review with Peter what his long-term goals are. Discuss.
- Guide Peter in analyzing which of his behavior patterns are conducive to reaching his goals and which he sees as impeding him from reaching them. Discuss what needs to change for him to reach his goals faster and more productively.
- If relevant, ask Peter whether and how the negative perceptions in the Coworker Action Research Report are hindering him from reaching his desired goals.

- Have Peter do a SWOT analysis of his career (i.e., an organized list of his strengths, weaknesses, opportunities, and threats).
- Ask Peter to decide what negative perceptions he wants to change and how best to leverage his strengths.
- Help Peter identify quick and easy action steps he can implement immediately to address the negative perceptions.
- Work with him to identify any consequences or threats of not tackling an issue before he decides not to address a negative perception that might hurt his career.
- Explore with Peter different assumptions about why stakeholders have these negative perceptions of him. Drill down to very specific behaviors or attitudes that project these negative perceptions.
- Explore with Peter the deeper issues underlying his angry outbursts, to develop his self-awareness and insight and address some of his unmet underlying needs.
- Help him learn to manage negative perceptions and develop strategies to counter those perceptions.
- Review and identify how best to leverage his strengths in different business contexts.

"Lauren, how exactly will you develop Peter's self-awareness?" inquired Amanda.

"I will read the report with him, asking him why he thinks people feel or say these things about him. Peter will produce his theory. I expect he'll tell me his critics are lazy and incompetent and accuse them of under-performing. He'll perceive them as hindering him, and he'll attack. The coach's work is to help Peter understand the cost this behavior has on his relationships and longer term goals."

Lauren continued, frowning slightly. "Initially, Peter may not realize his contribution to his employees' lack of engagement. As Peter's coaches, we want to develop his emotional intelligence using what he has—an abundance of IQ and a strong drive for results. My job is to have him identify what other underlying issues might be at play, but we are unlikely to accomplish that in the first debriefing meeting. He will probably be dealing with the shock of learning how people perceive him. He'll be on a roller coaster—he'll fluctuate from elation and relief as he reads about his strengths to shock at the pain he has been causing. He will feel totally misunderstood. It is always painful to see someone in angst. If what he learns about how people perceive him is too painful and surprising to him, he might react emotionally," explained Lauren.

Glancing at her Swiss watch, Lauren started gathering up her papers. It was time for her meeting with Peter. "I'll meet back up with you later to let you know how our session goes," she told Amanda as she headed out the door.

DEBRIEFING THE COWORKER ACTION RESEARCH REPORT

Lauren knocked on Peter's office door an hour on the dot after he came storming into her office. Peter greeted her congenially at the door and invited her to take a seat at his conference table. This was a completely different Peter from an hour ago. He was charming and inviting.

No sooner did she sit down than Peter said to her, "I need you to fix this situation. There is a board meeting next month, and I will be presenting my strategy for the Asian market. I'll need the board to approve excess resources to make it happen. I want these rumors about me addressed by then." Peter spoke with his familiar persuasive charm, the opposite of the agitation and rudeness she'd seen earlier.

"Peter, we first need to find out what exactly these rumors are. The Coworker Action Research Report Amanda and I have compiled will provide us with this information. I invite you to go through it with me. This is the most challenging part of the coaching process." Lauren paused and looked at Peter to gauge his emotional state.

"Come on, give it to me straight. I've handled more difficult situations than this before," Peter answered defiantly.

"What I recommend is that we read through it once together. I've taken out anything that would identify the commenter, so sometimes the meaning might be difficult to understand. I am here to give it context, but without naming anyone. So please refrain from asking me who said what, as I shall not answer."

Lauren handed Peter his Coworker Action Research Report and asked whether he wanted to read the report.

"No, no, no, you read it," replied Peter. He seemed reluctant even to take the document from her.

Debriefing With the Client

1. Debrief patterns and categories with the client. Help him or her develop a tentative hypothesis about the cause of the feedback.
2. Identify with the client what behaviors he or she will change to get a better reaction and perception from respondents, and reduce the gap between the client's goals and the current challenges.
3. If a client is resistant to change, review the possible consequences of not addressing the behavior.
4. Begin with the easiest behavior changes for immediate results.
5. Once the first changes have been made, coach the client on the selected behavior changes that remain and are more challenging.
6. Evaluate the stakeholders' perceptions of the client's changes six months later.

Lauren began by reading aloud the comments about Peter's strengths. He was visibly pleased at what he was hearing, but also obviously apprehensive about what was coming next. His body had stiffened, and he was fiddling nervously with his pen. As Lauren began reading what respondents felt would make their relationship with Peter more productive, the pen actually came apart in his fingers. Lauren let this pass without comment and continued reading.

"'He lacks sensitivity,'" she read aloud. "'He is untactful in the way he says things.'"

Peter moved uncomfortably in his chair, then burst out in anger, "I don't care what they think; the job needs to be done, and it only gets done when I whip them into shape. I am not here to take care of their feelings. It's not my job."

A long silence followed, until Peter said, "Read on!" with authority. He listened quietly again until Lauren read, "'He does not set clear expectations.'"

"I tell them what to do until I am blue in the face. But they are incompetent. Stupid!" vociferated Peter.

"Can you think of any other reason why they have this perception?" countered Lauren, thinking to herself that some of his direct reports might be too scared to ask for clarifications. She immediately regretted her words, though. It was too early to ask probing questions that required him to think—he was too emotionally upset. She needed to give him time and was glad it was late Friday afternoon. Peter would have the weekend to cool down. She had already set an appointment in his agenda for early Monday morning. She had also checked with him beforehand to make sure he had no major business decisions to make in his current emotional state.

Luckily for Lauren, Peter ignored her question and kept glancing down the page to see what was coming next. Lauren started reading again to pace the feedback process and gauge Peter's reactions. When she came to the end of the report, she looked up at Peter again. He was shaking, silent, and too hurt to have another outburst.

"Just give me the answers, Lauren," Peter said firmly but in a steady voice, trying to conceal his emotion.

Lauren knew she needed to always ask questions, not try to fix the immediate problem. She told Peter soothingly, "We need to understand what specific behaviors, attitudes, or opinions you have that cause people to develop these perceptions about you. This is work we will be doing together, because I don't know you as well as you do, and you can't change your behavior in just one meeting. Take the weekend, reread the report, and pick the categories you want to work on first."

Lauren reminded herself of the importance of showing Peter that she did not need to have all the answers for him. Instead, her attitude should convey to Peter, "We need to try to understand this together"— even though when she saw him in pain, she wanted desperately to come to his rescue.

Lauren continued comfortingly, "Our objective is to understand why your stakeholders have these perceptions and what we can do so that they improve or disappear. Decide what section you want to work on first and why. When we come back together on Monday, I'll ask you about your thoughts, feelings, and reactions on each section. For now, we will identify together a few quick action steps you can implement to improve the situation." Lauren was intentionally taking the lead in the conversation to reassure an unsettled Peter.

Unusually silent and contrite, Peter asked, "Is it possible to change in a month?" His hands were shaking while he stared at the report incredulously.

"Yes, you can change behaviors in a month, but it is difficult. It will depend on you!" said Lauren, not forgetting that Peter was a predator and would rise to the challenge even if he felt like prey today. Even though she knew that it might take a few months to achieve sustainable change in behavior, having a difficult goal to work toward should help keep Peter motivated and putting in the needed effort.

THE COACHING ACTION PLAN PROCESS STARTS

Early Monday morning, before the working day started to buzz with energy, Lauren came into the Tempus office, made herself a coffee, and walked toward Peter's office. She thought after reviewing the quick action steps with Peter, the critical part of the coaching would be having him generate theories about why others react to him the way they do and helping him broaden his perspective. As his coach, Lauren would explore different theories with him. After all, Lauren and Peter were co-researchers.[i]

After each coaching session, she would encourage him to draw up an action plan to test his assumptions and try out different behaviors. Then, at the following session, they would discuss his results and the reactions he had gotten. She knew she was only a facilitator, and to pave the way for Peter, she had diligently coached the key stakeholders about how to help make their relationship with Peter more productive. Peter would initially learn from her, but she needed to be sure that the improved communication among key stakeholders continued once she was no longer his coach.

Lauren saw that Peter's office door was open. He heard her coming and immediately stood up and welcomed her into the office.

"Have a seat," he said smiling. He had completely regained his composure over the weekend and showed no signs of his nervousness on Friday. "Here are my quick action steps," Peter said as he handed her his paper, visibly engaged and interested in the process. Lauren started reading.

---

i   The concept of the coach and client as co-researchers comes from Laura Crawshaw's Boss Whispering approach.

- I want to listen more to people instead of finger-pointing.
  I want to engage people instead of forcing them to comply.

- I need to admit when I'm tired and need a break
  (it's not a sin).

Lauren wondered where Peter's drive came from. Might it have started in childhood, when he competed with his brothers for parental attention? She would ask open-ended questions at some point in their coaching conversation to explore this possibility, only because it might help Peter to identify situations when his anger might erupt.

- Focus on a few key projects and doing them well instead of trying to do everything.

"Hmm," thought Lauren, "he plans to focus on quality rather than quantity and relieve some of the pressure on himself to be the best in every domain. What is the cause of that constant pressure on him to always accept more work?" she wondered. "He will need to discern what to take on and what not to. He'll need to clarify what quality means to him and determine how to decrease his workload. Hmm, we will likely need to work on developing some strategies for him and discuss how to say no to projects in the appropriate manner. Interpersonally, he will need to be more accepting of his own and others' human vulnerabilities and frailties."

- Perception—what other people think or take away from an interaction—is what is important.

Lauren was especially pleased with this quick action step. "How wonderful that he is not debating whether what people say is true and that he accepts the importance of perceptions," she thought to herself. "We will work on the potential gap between his intent and others' perceptions."

- Stop feeling guilty when I say no. Everyone's demands push me to the limit, which is when I'm most vulnerable to "outbursts."

Lauren pondered where this guilt came from. Why must Peter always outperform others? She needed to ask him what he thought there was to be guilty about. What was the underlying anxiety? If he underperforms, what is he guilty of—inadequacy, stupidity, or laziness? Lauren knew that Peter felt threatened by overwhelming performance demands and seemed to be projecting his own subconscious fear of incompetence onto others by yelling and attacking them.

"But," she wondered, "where does this insecurity come from, and how might Peter come to realize it?"

- When I feel I am ignored or not recognized, I need to reassure myself that I'm okay.

Lauren thought she needed to ask Peter during the next coaching session why it was so hard for him to feel ignored. When did he first start having those feelings in his life? Did they go back to the days when Peter's father ignored him in favor of his more athletic brothers? Were the hurts of his childhood being played out at work? Peter would benefit from understanding the source of this extreme sensitivity to being ignored. It would help him to develop a strategy for how best to handle his anxieties.

"As his coach," thought Lauren, "my role is to make him aware of the options he has in handling and responding to a situation that he perceives as a threat to his self-perception. It is important for Peter to monitor his immediate response to situations, then develop options for how to react to different situations in the most human but also strategic way."

- Don't go into overdrive, or try to force the issue, or overcompensate. My reaction or response may be perceived negatively. Be aware when this happens.

"It is important for Peter to know that he has choices in the way he reacts," thought Lauren. "He might have only a nanosecond to decide how to react, but in that very brief moment, if he can stop and think before reacting impulsively, he can decide what will get him what he wants without destroying the relationship. Over the long term, does it serve his goals to force compliance or stimulate engagement? This shift in approach would be difficult initially for Peter."

Lauren wanted Peter to know he could let off steam with her instead of his stakeholders, at least initially, until they could identify together less destructive ways of reacting. The goal was to analyze the situation together and come up with more productive ways of reacting that would get Peter what he wanted in both the short term and the longer term, as well as engage his followers. This would require a behavior change and would take some time to learn. Peter needed to develop his emotional intelligence—that is, he needed to learn to monitor and manage his own emotions and respond more appropriately to the emotions of others. Until he developed more awareness, the monitoring might not help him control his emotions, but it was an essential first step before he could manage his and other's emotions productively.

After some thinking, Lauren asked Peter when he first noticed that he went into overdrive and forced issues. Peter looked down at the floor for what felt like a long time, then raised his eyes to Lauren and spoke.

"My athletic brothers were always the apple of my parents' eye. When I did not achieve what the family expected of me, my brothers humiliated me and at times beat me up. My parents never defended me against their bullying. I was always compared to my brothers' outstanding achievements and chastened for my lack of physical ability. Failing was not an option."

"It's important for parents to love their children for what they do," thought Lauren, "but it is equally or even more important to simply love them for who they are." Not being a psychologist, Lauren wouldn't lead Peter deeper into this issue, but she would have a referral handy in case it seemed necessary. For the time being, Lauren thought, the issue could probably be resolved through a customized coaching process.

"Can I change?" asked Peter, interrupting Lauren's thoughts. His body was slightly stooped, and he seemed to be shaking.

"I cannot change your past," she answered him reassuringly, "but we can work on developing your awareness and your choices about how to react, which will provide you with more options for the future. Your drive to achieve has made you successful in the past, but without change, it might be the seed of your derailment in the future."

Peter looked worried, but Lauren continued, "Through insight, which includes a deeper awareness of your deep-seated needs, motivation, values, and anxieties, you will learn to see situations differently. A change of behavior will be the outcome, and encouraging results will drive you to continue to change," she commented softly, with as much empathy as she could convey.

Lauren then asked Peter, "Reading through the Coworker Action Research Report, you must have felt a series of different emotions. I should have told you ahead of time that this was to be expected and normal," she said, although she had not had any hope of communicating this to him at their last meeting, given how upset he was.

Peter paused and sighed before answering, "I am not completely surprised by the Coworker Action Research Report. I have received such feedback before, but what is hurtful is that people think I am not trustworthy and I'm only out for myself. They don't see how hard I work for John and the company in general."

Privately, Lauren wondered, "Might he work so hard for the company to get the recognition he feels he deserves? Does Peter want to surpass John's accomplishments because he sees John as a fatherly figure, or are there other reasons?"

Lauren thought the better of sharing such questions with Peter. Instead, she asked him, "What do you want to work on first from your list of action points?"

"I want to listen to people more instead of finger-pointing. I want to engage people instead of forcing them to comply," answered Peter.

"Bright fellow," thought Lauren. "He is focusing on the perceptions of others, which is the core of the matter."

Aloud, she reformulated his words. "If I understand correctly, Peter, you want to be a better listener, not start conversations by blaming people, and develop a leadership style that engages people rather than forcing them to comply."

"That is exactly it," agreed Peter.

"Peter, are you ready to work hard between coaching sessions?"

"Yes," he answered with determination. "Let's move forward quickly."

"I am going to ask you to take several actions steps between now and our next coaching session," continued Lauren. "First, I want you to identify what you feel and think just before you explode with anger. Observe yourself as a researcher, and when you are calmer, write down what just happened to you, how you reacted, and what you felt. In our next coaching session, we will go through what you tell yourself when going into defense mode."

"I can do that," Peter replied.

"I also want you to read an article by Daniel Goleman, 'Leadership That Gets Results.' I want you to identify which of the six leadership styles you use most and what leadership style you want to develop to engage people instead of commanding them. We will build a repertoire of leadership styles, so that you can adapt your leadership style to the person and context more effectively and easily. Together, we will analyze what leadership situations you are in, what are the outcome and goals you want, and how best to engage the person you are working with. Then we will identify what leadership style is most appropriate in which situation."

Lauren handed Peter a copy of the article by Goleman, which she'd brought along with her to the meeting.

"There is one more thing I want you to do before our next meeting," she continued. "Peter, the human mind thinks between 500 and 800 words a minute, and the speed at which people talk is roughly around 125 to 150 words a minute. Therefore, it's hard to stay focused on another person's words without thinking or multitasking in your head.

"What I want you to do is keep your mind focused on the other person instead of thinking about what you are going to say or do next. To help you, I have an exercise that will help you get to know the other person better. It is a series of useful questions that you must get answers to without asking the questions directly. The information you gather will also help you adapt your leadership style to specific people, so that your relationship is even more productive for both of you."

This seemed like a lot for Peter to absorb in his emotional state, so Lauren offered a bit more explanation.

"Peter, the other day when you, John, and I had lunch, I noticed that in those forty minutes, you interrupted John four times to bring the conversation back to you. Do you remember when John was talking about how his family always vacations in the same place so his wife can bring along their two dogs? He said he wished they could take more adventurous vacations instead. He was joking that the dogs' happiness was more important to his wife than his. Then, Peter, you interrupted him to describe the attributes of your dog. The issue was not the dogs but that John felt his vacation needs were not being met and that he felt his wife was putting more importance on the dogs' needs than on his."

Peter looked taken aback as Lauren gave her other three examples.

"What are you looking for when you so frequently bring the conversation back to yourself?" enquired Lauren soothingly.

"His attention," replied Peter rapidly.

"Might there be a better way to get his attention? How could you get his full attention and keep the subject on him?"

"I could have asked him about his dogs!"

"How could you have shown your concern for John?" solicited Lauren, knowing that she was exploring areas that were in Peter's blind spot.

Peter did not respond. He just looked down at his papers, then back to her expectantly. After a long silence, he suddenly blurted out, "I could have asked questions or at least responded to what he was saying and what he was not saying?" Peter looked at Lauren inquisitively to determine whether he was on the right track. "I could have asked him if he was having problems with his wife. But my job isn't to hold people's hands— I'm here to get work done."

"Yet I observed over lunch that you brought the subject back to your personal issues and not to subjects about work," countered Lauren. "Let's take an out-of-context example. Have you ever bought a car from a pushy salesman you couldn't stand?" asked Lauren. "People will more readily work with those they like and have developed a relationship with. Is that the same for you?"

"Yes, I get your point. I see how I kept pulling the subject back to my issues and wasn't sensitive to his situation. I could have just listened and asked questions, or asked him what problems he was having with his wife."

"Those are definitely options. You might want to wait until John explicitly mentions his problem with his wife before asking him such a direct and personal question. That would come across as less intrusive, especially since I was present and don't have such a personal relationship with him," said Lauren, thinking that Peter was catching on very quickly, even if he was a little abrupt.

"Given that you want to learn to listen more, I have an exercise that might help," added Lauren. She reached for a piece of paper and drew a little man with a head, body, two arms, and two legs, then she drew a heart at the torso and a circle at the gut. She drew a line from the man's head to the left side of the paper and wrote, "What is John thinking?" Next she drew a line from the man's hands and wrote on the side of the paper, "What does John want to do? What are his dreams?" Then she drew a line from his heart to the side of the paper and wrote, "What are his passions?" Lauren did the same with the gut, but this time wrote, "What are John's fears?" For the legs, Lauren wrote, "Where does John want to go? What are his career aspirations?"

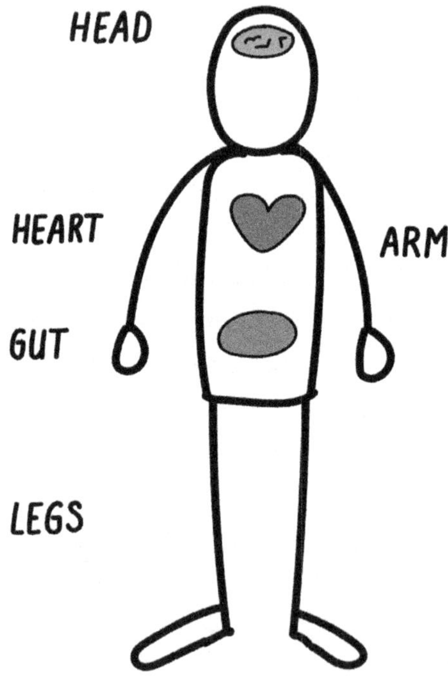

"Do you know the answers to these questions, Peter?" she asked.

Peter was silent for so long that Lauren asked the question again, thinking he might not have heard her. Finally, Peter slowly answered each one of Lauren's questions. She kept asking probing questions along the way until Peter described John's assumptions, passions, fears, and needs in detail. Lauren listened in silence, pleased by how insightful Peter's answers were becoming.

Lauren noticed how amazed Peter was about how much information he was able to provide with Lauren's penetrating questions. She smiled and told him these were good assumptions, and now it was important that he verify his assumptions with regard to John, without being intrusive or too personal. Peter was not to ask any direct questions.

Lauren explained how to reformulate what someone says without repeating the words mechanically. "Reformulate the essence of what has been said, just enough to let the other person know that you understand what they are saying and that you are on the same page or not, if you disagree. When you reformulate what the person said, if you misunderstood anything, then he or she has the opportunity to correct any misinterpretations. It also helps the speaker clarify his or her own thoughts."

As an afterthought, Lauren added, "Do ask John's permission to do this exercise with him, and forewarn him that it is part of a coaching exercise. Then ask him for feedback on how you went about asking him questions—that is, what you did well and what you can do better. Are you comfortable doing this exercise, Peter?"

Lauren knew that Peter wanted to get closer to John, and this was one of the ways she thought he could do so. This was also a tangible way John could help Peter improve his interpersonal skills.

"Yes," answered Peter. "I'll do this exercise with John and with my direct reports. I can see how it might be useful to better understand my boss and employees, and how I might adapt what I say and my leadership style to the person I'm talking to," responded Peter, visibly enthusiastic about this new approach.

Lauren was also glad she had warned Peter's direct reports that they were going to be part of the process. She had told them that Peter's initial attempts might be a little awkward, but that they should see it as a desire to improve, which she knew it was.

While she was in his good graces, Lauren ventured to ask Peter, "Might you find out more about George using the 'little man' questions indirectly? We could debrief it in our next coaching session and compare perspectives."

"Maybe, but not now," replied Peter dismissively.

Lauren was going to push back a bit, but then decided it was more important at this stage of the coaching process to ask Peter for John's feedback. She ventured, "John offered to provide you with helpful feedback on a regular basis. How would you feel about asking him to offer you his observations after major meetings and asking him the same questions: What did you do well during the meeting managing peers and team members, and what could you improve?"

"Won't I appear a little juvenile asking him such questions? I have been leading for years," countered Peter.

"I see it more as an opportunity to know John's key performance indicators: what you do well and what he thinks you could do better when handling people. He is extremely good with people. He is a good diplomat and politically able. He can serve as a mentor, but, additionally, you can take this opportunity to share your vision and strategy and talk to him like a peer. This interaction will also help him observe the progress you are making firsthand. I am not present in your daily business activities. You need to find people you trust who are willing to provide you with honest feedback immediately after an event," remarked Lauren.

"Okay, will do. I know who I am going to ask," asserted Peter.

"Peter, I also want to manage expectations. In this two-hour meeting, we have now tackled the first priority you suggested. How long do you think it will take to address all your objectives?" asked Lauren.

"Okay, Lauren, I understand that it will take longer than a month to address these issues, but how long will it take before key stakeholders observe some changes in me?"

"It is difficult to say, but most probably, the key stakeholders will notice some of your behavior changes in less than a month."

Lauren and Peter finished the coaching session by going over the key action items Peter would implement or try out before his next coaching session. Lauren asked him what he had learned from this session. What were the key items Peter wanted to work on that he could share with his team? He needed to thank everyone who had participated in the Coworker Action Research Report. If Peter had the courage, he could share with the participants some of the items he was going to work on and let them know he would be asking them for feedback.

Both feeling good about all they had accomplished that day, Peter and Lauren scheduled their next appointment, and she left him to get back to his workday. As she left his office, she gave him a warm smile. She was going to enjoy working with Peter.

Chapter Review Questions

1. What did you notice about Lauren's style of coaching Peter?
2. What did you like or dislike in the way Lauren coached Peter?
3. Which of Lauren's techniques would you apply in your coaching or in your leadership role?
4. How long do you think it would take Peter to change his ways? What would you expect to be easy or difficult for him?

CHAPTER 15

INTEGRATING THE COACHING PROCESS

Sustainable Change for the Abrasive Jerk and the Organization

---

Lauren knew the action items were easy enough for Peter to conceive, but the challenge was in implementing them in the moment, while under pressure to perform. She was impressed with his determination and drive, and looked forward to watching him put the steps to work.

INTEGRATING CHANGE INTO THE CLIENT'S DAILY LIFE

A few days after their first session, on a sunny summer afternoon, Lauren shut herself in her office to write an important and urgent report. She asked her assistant to block all her calls so that she could get the report finished for the meeting with the members of the board the following day. Suddenly, she heard a knock on her door. Before she had a chance to answer, the door burst open, and Peter marched in, visibly upset.

"I must talk to you!" he insisted.

Lauren's assistant stood just behind Peter, signaling to Lauren apologetically that she had tried to stop him but couldn't. Lauren nodded almost imperceptibly to indicate that it was okay. She would handle it. Her assistant, relieved, closed the door behind Peter.

"Have a seat, Peter," said Lauren, gesturing in the direction of the chair in front of her desk. Peter flopped down onto the big, black leather chair, noticeably dejected.

"What's up?" asked Lauren.

"I was having a pleasant lunch with my colleague Jean-Marc. We were discussing sports and business in general and having a great time together. At 2pm, we had a meeting we needed to attend together to resolve a business development issue we are having in China. But when I saw Tempus's chairman seated at the meeting table, I found myself arguing every proposal Jean-Marc made during the meeting.

"My points were flawless, but Jean-Marc looked at me in shock, and I could tell he was hurt by my cutting and incisive remarks. He started losing his concentration and becoming flustered, because my comments made his suggestions seem unfounded. Jean-Marc lost face.....No, *I made* him lose face. Lauren, I couldn't help myself," Peter said quietly. He fell silent and looked down at the papers in front of him, disheartened.

Lauren broke the silence by asking, "What did you want to prove to the chairman?"

"I wanted my plan to win. I wanted the chairman to see I was the better leader."

"Did he?" inquired Lauren.

"Yes," Peter answered resolutely.

"What do you assume he thought of how you went about it?" continued Lauren.

"He thought I was ruthless," answered Peter.

"How do you know?" asked Lauren.

"A few times, the chairman came to Jean-Marc's rescue by underlining some of his positive arguments," remarked Peter. "I think he felt sorry for him."

"What is the consequence of winning in such a way, Peter?" queried Lauren gently.

"Jean-Marc will never trust me again," retorted Peter.

"So the cost was your friendship with Jean-Marc?" reformulated Lauren. "What were you trying to gain?"

Peter was silent for several moments and seemed to be in a daze. Then he said slowly, in a low voice, "I know, I wanted the chairman's recognition, Lauren. But I couldn't help myself . . . I couldn't." His voice was full of despair.

"Were you aware of what you were doing while you were competing with Jean-Marc?" questioned Lauren.

"Yes . . . yes, I was," answered Peter, obviously still visualizing the scene in the boardroom.

"These are the most difficult moments, Peter, when you are aware but still not able to change your ways," empathized Lauren. "Can you think of other times when appreciation has seemed so important to you?"

Peter paused a long time, looking straight past Lauren into the distance. "When I used to argue with my brothers to get my dad's praise. My brothers were talented athletes, and I could not compete at that level. I just couldn't, despite my continuous efforts. But I could outsmart them, and I did."

"Peter, it seems you have a strong need for recognition. Might you doubt your own self-worth?" questioned Lauren.

"Okay, okay, so I relentlessly want to prove myself," he admitted grudgingly.

"If you don't internalize your worth and celebrate your successes," Lauren said, "you might believe you are only as good as your last performance."

Peter paused for a moment, weighing the significance of Lauren's words, then nodded in agreement.[i]

"What were you apprehensive about in the meeting with the chairman?" continued Lauren.

"I was worried that the chairman might think Jean-Marc is more competent than I am or that he wouldn't notice me in the meeting." Peter fell silent and looked at his shoes again. "I am pretty screwed up, huh?" he said ruefully.

"This approach to get attention might have served you in the past with your brothers, but in the current situation, it is detrimental to your friendships and to your image as an engaging leader for the company. How might have you said what you think without destroying Jean-Marc's confidence?" probed Lauren.

"Let him present first and not interrupt?" answered Peter lamely.

"What else?" probed Lauren, thinking it would likely be difficult for Peter to refrain from interrupting.

"I don't know . . . not say anything?" answered Peter, at a loss.

"How might you have earned the chairman's recognition that you are a good leader while keeping Jean-Marc's trust?"

"Give him a chance to problem-solve?" continued Peter. "What do you think, Lauren?"

---

i   Kaplan classified insecure abrasive leaders into three subtypes. The first is the *striver–builder*, whose insecurity and drive for success stem from an underlying desire to fulfill his or her parents' expectations of greatness. The second subtype, *self-vindicator/fix-it specialist*, is driven to redeem himself or herself in the eyes of parents who were cold or rejecting. Finally, the *perfectionist–systematizer* strives to gain the approval of perfectionistic parents. Given Peter's history, he is likely a striver–builder (R. E. Kaplan, *Beyond Ambition: How Driven Managers Can Lead Better and Live Better.* San Francisco: Jossey-Bass, 1991).

Lauren kept silent and waited for Peter to come up with the answers on his own.

"I could have exposed the flaws in Jean-Marc's arguments but excused him because he does not know the company well enough yet. This would have helped Jean-Marc save face."

"Yes, and what other missed opportunities were there?"

"I could have used the moment to show how I can help a peer develop. It is in my best interest to counter my reputation for being 'uncivil' in the workplace," concluded Peter with a sarcastic smile.

"May I share my observations?" asked Lauren.

"I want you to," answered Peter, straightening up in his chair and looking at her with interest.

"Yes, showing how you help a peer would have helped your reputation. It would have exhibited another aspect of your leadership. It would have illustrated that you are dedicated to maximizing the company's overall results and not just your own. It would have shown you as a team player and ready to brainstorm with colleagues in a constructive way.

Observing your interactions in other meetings, Peter, I have noticed that you systematically start with what is *not* working. Although it is a talent to see where things can go wrong before others do, it can also be demotivating for enthusiasts who are eager to get the project started. So what about starting conversations with what *is* working, and only then address what can be improved? This will get them thinking. Be sure to use the word *and*, not *but*, so that you're indicating what can be added and improved rather than countering other people's ideas," added Lauren to jump-start his thinking.

"Add to his argument, or ask him how he might address my concerns within his plan, to give him a chance to problem-solve?" repeated Peter. "But if his proposal and approach are mistaken, he should know it," he insisted stubbornly.

"What is your desired final outcome, Peter?" Lauren persisted. "To prove that you are right in your reasoning and Jean-Marc is wrong, or to strengthen Jean-Marc's thinking, coax him to address your observations, and move the whole organization forward in the same direction? What would a CEO of the organization do?"

"I didn't think of that," Peter said. "You mean instead of attacking Jean-Marc's argumentation, I could help him strengthen his ideas by providing him with 'what if' situations. For example, 'If x were to occur, how would you handle y?' Prevent him from making what I think are errors, but propose them as suggestions instead of attacks? . . . Yes, I can do that."

"What opportunity did you miss to show the chairman that you are a leader with the company's overall interest at heart?" asked Lauren.

"It would have been an opportunity to demonstrate that I am a people builder," stated Peter. "What do you think of me, Lauren?" he asked hesitantly after a moment.

"As I see it Peter, you are not intentionally mean, but you have unmet needs and fears. You might see situations as more threatening than most leaders under similar stress would. Let me state the obvious, Peter. If you had enough confidence in yourself, you would not have felt threatened by Jean-Marc's statements. A new recruit, like Jean-Marc—is he really a challenge to your competence?" questioned Lauren.

Peter pondered Lauren's words. "Okay, I will go talk to Jean-Marc and apologize," he said.

"That's a start, but it might take more than that to regain his trust," she mused.

"What should I do?" queried Peter.

"What do you suggest?" countered Lauren. She wanted to make him think about it before giving him any suggestions.

"Jean-Marc is a friend. I will apologize to him, then share with him that I am going through a coaching program and that what I did to him in the meeting is precisely what I am trying to work on changing. He is in most of my meetings, and he is a person I trust to give me straight feedback—if he is still willing after today's debacle," answered Peter, obviously embarrassed to have to apologize and make himself so vulnerable.

"Do I have to have someone checking on me in team meetings and providing me with feedback?" he asked. "I will feel policed."

"It is a good idea to get as much feedback as possible from people you trust until your new behaviors have become habits. It also helps stakeholders notice the improvements you make. Progress usually does not happen in a straight line. Under stressful situations, you might be tempted to relapse into your old ways, but if you increase your insight and keep working toward a better understanding of yourself, you will gain more self-control and find more constructive ways of releasing your frustrations and perceived threats."

"I guess that makes sense."

"This leadership development program will give you an opportunity to leverage your IQ, which you have plenty of, and further develop your EQ to build your interpersonal relationships and attract engaged followers. This is aligned with your long-term goal to become the CEO of this company. Keep in mind, Peter, as CEO, you would be responsible not only for your division but for the company as a whole, with all its stakeholders."

Peter nodded in understanding, and Lauren continued, "The coaching process cannot compensate for your need to be recognized by key individuals in your life, but it can provide you with a better understanding of what triggers your frustrations and help you find better and more constructive ways to deal with your defensive outbursts when you perceive threats to your self-esteem," stated Lauren. "Or your insecurities," she thought but did not say.

There was a knock on the door, and Lauren's assistant popped her head in. "Your next appointment is here, Lauren!" she said, and then immediately ducked back out and closed the door behind her, apprehensive of how Peter might react to her interrupting a confidential discussion.

Peter got up to walk toward the door, then, quickly, as if he had forgotten something, turned around, and said, "Thank you. This was helpful."

"You are welcome, Peter," answered Lauren, flashing a caring smile. With a quick look at her watch, she realize the hour to write her report had passed, but her meeting with Peter had been important and productive. It was worth the time lost, she thought. Her next appointment with him was scheduled for the following week, and she was eager to see what improvements he might make in the meantime.

CORE COMPETENCIES FOR EMPLOYEE REVIEWS

As Peter stepped out, George walked into Lauren's office. The two men greeted each other politely but with reserve.

"So how is the coaching coming along with Peter?" asked George after closing Lauren's office door.

"It's going well," answered Lauren, careful not to reveal anything personal about Peter, through either her words or her body language. She knew she had an expressive face, so she looked away and started searching for a pen.

"How have you found Peter this last week?" inquired Lauren as she rummaged in her drawer. With a deliberately blank expression, she put the pen on her desk and faced George.

"I can see he has been trying to be more cordial with me or avoid me completely," answered George.

"At this stage in the change process, coachees might not know how to respond to people differently than they used to. They might feel awkward with people or avoid them altogether until they are more comfortable using new behaviors. When coachees withdraw from you, they are using the flight strategy rather than dealing with their discomfort at handling a situation differently. They no longer know how to respond. They have left their old ways but have not yet fully integrated new behaviors.

"In Peter's case, the change will come, George. I know I can count on you to be patient and tactful but truthful when he does come around to try to establish a better relationship with you," added Lauren. "Now let's get back to our reason for meeting. We need to discuss the new procedures we're putting in place for employees' reviews."

"Before we do, I just want to share with you that Peter asked me to have lunch with him this coming week," interjected George, smiling and visibly pleased.

"That's great news," Lauren said. "Okay, George, let's review the competencies we need to develop within the organization to reach Tempus's long-term goals and mission. As we agreed, this list of competencies will now serve as the basis for the performance review process, to bring it more in line with what we want to develop in our leaders to meet the needs of the organization in the coming years."

Lauren was anxious to make this change, given that Frank had asked her to lead the annual and semiannual performance reviews.

"George, we both know the customized Coworker Action Research Assessment is too onerous for everyone in the company to go through. So, instead, Tempus will use this list of desired competencies and behaviors when evaluating employees for the semiannual performance reviews and for the 360-Degree Feedback Reports," stated Lauren as she handed George the list of desired competencies agreed on by the executive committee.

Lauren thought to herself that she would review these behaviors with Peter in her next meeting so that he could identify more specifically what he wanted to work on that was directly linked to the company's desired behaviors and competencies.

"By the way, George, this report, together with what was discussed in the triad meeting for Peter's leadership development program, will be used as his desired benchmark during the triad meeting with you and John in three months," asserted Lauren.

"Yes, we agreed on that," acquiesced George.

Then Lauren turned back to the ten competencies, which would be assessed through a competency-based questionnaire or through interviews. Each competency was clearly defined with specific descriptors, to make it easier for managers to evaluate the degree to which these behaviors were demonstrated by the employee.[ii]

---

ii   Competencies assessments are common organizational frameworks used to evaluate desired behaviors in annual or semiannual performance appraisals.

Core Values of the Competencies Assessment

- Integrity and sensitivity to diversity
- Leadership behaviors (strategic thinking, decision making, planning and organizing, and leading change)
- Personal qualities (building partnerships, working with others, and communicating with influence)

The information contained in this document would serve as a framework for discussion among the employee concerned, the line management, and the employee's direct reports. It could be used to highlight areas to focus the employee's broader development as well as to set any specific development activities and targets.

A 360-Degree Feedback Report can be too time-consuming for semiannual employee reviews. A clearly defined Competencies Assessment serves as a better way to evaluate leaders and coworkers.

George and Lauren worked on tweaking the Competencies Assessment for two hours before both were satisfied with the outcome. Lauren had already picked out several of the behaviors to discuss with Peter in her next session. She quickly skimmed the rest of the document to determine where Peter could brainstorm how to improve. Leadership and working with others were the areas Lauren assumed Peter needed to focus on. She would discuss this with him, together with the Coworker Action Research Report results.

Competencies Assessment for Use in Employee Reviews

Decision Making

- Analyzes problems to reach specific, evidence-based decisions
- Evaluates the pros and cons of options and the impact of decisions
- Accepts responsibility for own decisions; makes tough decisions

Leadership

- Inspires, motivates, and guides others to accomplish key goals
- Empowers others, promoting mutual trust and commitment
- Sets clear performance expectations and provides feedback
- Manages poor performance constructively; provides coaching and development

Working With Others

- Understands, shows sensitivity toward, and cares for others
- Listens to others and works in an inclusive, tactful manner
- Enjoys others' company and interacts openly and respectfully
- Is resilient and manages own emotions effectively in interactions

Lauren would also have Peter complete psychometric and personality inventories (e.g., the Myers–Briggs Type Indicator, Belbin Team Inventory) to evaluate his preferred style of behavior, his way of making decisions, and his way of dealing with stress. It would be helpful to determine how Peter expressed his creative style, his preferred leadership styles, and the leadership styles he wanted to develop further.

Lauren always felt that any psychometric inventory should be used as a platform of discussion rather than a means to categorize people or evaluate them. To avoid the risk of pigeonholing people, she preferred to use several inventories to see what attributes were mentioned repeatedly. Lauren was also curious to notice the different perspectives each inventory might highlight for Peter to develop his self-awareness. These inventories would allow Peter to think about certain of his attributes and better decipher other people's preferences. They would also allow him to use the framework to more consciously adapt his communication for maximum impact.

SIX MONTHS LATER

Competencies Assessment

Lauren had just finished another coaching session with Peter, and although it was not quite noon, she decided to walk to the canteen for an early lunch. She was deep in thought when she saw Amanda in line at the fish station. Lauren walked briskly to join her in the queue for fresh grilled fish. Amanda flashed a big smile at Lauren when she saw her.

"Lauren, good to see you. I have to tell you that I saw Peter at the new project kickoff meeting this morning. I can't believe the change I saw in his behavior when he was interacting with his team. He started the meeting by making positive remarks and complimenting his team's achievements. He even gave specific examples of what he appreciated. The 'old Peter' never did that! He even used his quick wit to tease George and asked George to stop him if he pushed his team too hard. I have never seen Peter so relaxed and pleasant in a meeting. He spent a good length of time with his team coaching them. Wow! What a change, Lauren," exclaimed Amanda.

"Peter is very smart, and with the right information, he catches on quickly," asserted Lauren. "How are you getting along with the follow-up Coworker Action Research Report, Amanda? Where you able to interview the same participants from the first report?"

"Yes. Although it took time out of their busy agendas, they were delighted to comply," answered Amanda. "I was surprised Peter agreed that I write up the Coworker Action Research Report instead of you. Seven months ago, he hardly considered me as a person. The stakeholders' feedback has radically improved, too."

Clearly, Amanda hadn't expected such a positive outcome. "Peter really rose to the challenge of changing his ways," she marveled. "I wasn't sure it was possible."

Lauren raised her eyebrows, "Peter still has more work to do, but his sincere interest in making changes has really helped him to progress."

When Lauren debriefed the second and last Coworker Action Research Report with Peter, she was impressed by how active and engaged he was in processing the information. Lauren hardly needed to say anything. Peter knew the process and actively brainstormed and questioned himself. When he read that he was still perceived as listening more to his in-group of direct reports, Lauren caught a brief glimpse of sadness in Peter's expression, but he quickly recognized what might have caused this perception and identified action steps to support his direct reports equally. With his heightened self-awareness and improved interpersonal understanding, Peter was quick to use his sharp mind to find solutions to the problems that arose. Amused, Lauren witnessed Peter integrating the coaching process and questioning himself.

Final Triad Meeting

The final step in the coaching process was to hold one more triad meeting among Peter, George, and John. On the day of the meeting, Peter walked into the room early and saw Lauren already there, standing by the window and looking out at the scenic view from the top-floor conference room. With his usual charm, he greeted her warmly. When George arrived, Peter chatted pleasantly with him, and when John walked into the room, Peter's face lit up.

John summoned them all to sit down at the conference table. Lauren took the lead and asked Peter to talk about the progress he felt he had made over the last six months and what might still remain to be worked on.

Peter thanked Lauren for her help, then listed several improvements he had made, and was quite harsh with himself about what he could still work harder on. George spoke next, but he had few improvements to suggest. He was pleased to finally have a good working relationship with Peter.

Lauren asked John to speak next. John had been Peter's main internal coach throughout the process. This had been Lauren's suggestion, because she felt Peter could benefit from emulating John's interpersonal ability and from receiving John's immediate feedback after meetings they had in common. John enumerated Peter's progress very specifically, with plenty of examples. He asked Peter to keep the good work up and implied that new possibilities within the company would open up to him with time.

Lauren looked over to Peter and saw him sighing with relief. He seemed content, relaxed, and simply happy. The recognition from John, Peter's trusted mentor, would go a long way to healing Peter's fears and insecurities.

Chapter Review Questions

1. What insights did Peter have during his discussion with Lauren, after the meeting with Tempus's chairman and his friend Jean Marc?
2. What new behavior was Lauren encouraging Peter to brainstorm about? Why?
3. Despite the progress he has made, in which situations might Peter relapse to his old ways?
4. Why is it best to use several inventories to determine employees' preferences instead of just one?

EPILOGUE

A YEAR LATER

At the General Assembly a year later, it was Peter's turn to give the annual results of his division and set the direction for the years to come. His speech was funny, witty, and strategic. He excited the crowd with his talent and charisma. He'd spoken well before, but this year something was different. He attributed credit to other people. He gave a witty but flattering homage to his boss, George, while teasing him kindly on his mannerisms. He rewarded and recognized his direct reports. The focus had shifted from *I* to *we*. He talked about the company at large, not only about his division. He acknowledged the contributions of other departments to his own department's successes.

Lauren had always admired Peter's wit and charm, but there was something so much more appealing about him this year. He was more human. She smiled when John Barbey walked up to him with a wrapped plaque.

Peter, taken by surprise, smiled and said, "So I got the booby prize this year?" but when he opened it, he was visibly moved. He had gotten the Best Leadership prize. And guess who had voted for him overwhelmingly? The coworkers in his division.

Lauren thought to herself, "Yes, achievers, brilliant and abrasive leaders—when they put their mind to it, who says they can't change? Abrasive jerks truly can become kind and thoughtful people." She smiled in her corner where no one could see her.

From across the room, Peter scanned the assembled crowd for her, and when he saw her, he gave her a beaming smile and winked.

God, did she love her job!

Appendix

The Excellent Executive Coaching Process to Inspire Brilliant Jerks to Be Brilliant Leaders

A s an external coach, the first contact you will have with a new client takes place when someone from the company asks you to develop their leaders. This request might come for one of several reasons—for help onboarding a new leader, for leadership development, or for remedial coaching. During this initial call, gather as much information as possible, and then send a coaching proposal to the organization. Then it is time to meet the leader you'll be coaching, to see whether the chemistry between the two of you gels.

As coaching progresses, you can follow the Excellent Executive Coaching Process as a guide. The Excellent Executive Coaching Process is summarized below.

FROM RESISTANCE TO ENGAGEMENT
Self-Awareness

STEP 1: EXPLORATORY MEETING: BUILD RAPPORT AND GAIN CLARITY

The purpose of the initial, exploratory meeting is to establish a trusting relationship with the client. This begins with the first meeting, the chemistry test. Intuitively and in general terms, the coach identifies the client's goals and challenges him or her to reach those goals. After this initial meeting, the potential client and the coach decide whether to work together. In the meantime, the coach draws on the discussion with the client to investigate the client's

- Personal and organizational goals
- Belief system and limiting beliefs
- Commitment to coaching and to change
- Strengths
- Mind-set
- Values
- Assumptions
- Motivation
- Biggest challenges
- Degree of defensiveness
- Ambition
- Fears
- Learning style
- Mental blocks or blind spots
- Incongruities
- Perception of coaching and the coach.

BYPASS DERAILMENT AND ALIGN EXPECTATIONS WITH THE BOSS
Boss Awareness

STEP 2: MEET WITH MANAGEMENT

Once you and the client have decided to work together, the next step is to meet or have a call with key management personnel. Use this meeting to determine what the client has been told about the need for change, the potential consequences of his or her behavior, and management's expectations for the coaching process. Inquire about the client's leadership behaviors and what the company values, what is taboo, and what the client must develop or alter, according to the stakeholders.

Preparing for the Triad Meeting Among the Boss, Client, and Coach

The triad meeting, which includes the client, his or her boss, the coach, and possibly a human resources representative, is an essential part of the Excellent Executive Coaching Process. To make sure all participants are fully prepared, take the following steps in advance of the meeting:

- Establish a coaching agreement that integrates the coaching agenda.
- Clearly indicate to stakeholders (mainly the client's immediate boss) that the coaching process is confidential.
- Identify key performance indicators.
- Identify the consequences the client will face if he or she does not change his or her behavior, as well as the benefits of change.
- Ensure that all parties agree about what support the client can expect from management and how much time he or she has to show changes in behavior.
- Assess how willing the client is to engage in a coaching process.
- Decide exactly what is to be communicated in any reports on the coaching process and when the next triad meeting will take place.
- Reinforce that all coaching conversations are confidential.

Triad Meeting

When leading the triad meeting, follow the steps below, in order, to ensure that the meeting remains constructive and provides the client plenty to work with as the coaching process progresses:

- Inform the meeting participants about the questions you will ask, and address any apprehension participants might have.
- Lead the discussion by asking questions such as the following:

- o "What would be a good outcome of this coaching program?"
  - o "What would you need to hear, feel, and see for the outcome to be good, bad, or excellent?"
  - o "What is the first improvement step you would expect to see?"
- Ask the client's boss what he or she will do to help the process (e.g., what event will the client and boss both attend, after which the client could receive immediate feedback about his or her leadership?).
- Observe interactions between stakeholders and the client, to compare perspectives later with the client during the coaching process.
- Encourage the bosses to express what they might have said in private to the coach, the consequences if the leader does not change his or her behaviors, and the benefits of behavior change. Keep the conversation constructive, keep dialogue flowing, and make sure the core issues surface. Expectations should be expressed in very explicit, tangible, and specific terms.
- Take notes on what is said during the meeting, for inclusion in the Coworker Action Research Report (see Chapters 11 and 12 for more on the Coworker Action Research Report).
- Reconfirm that the Coworker Action Research Report is for the client's eyes only. After the client has received the Coworker Action Research Report, encourage him or her to share with the boss areas he or she intends to work on and wants feedback on.
- Explain the flow of the coaching process, and note that another triad meeting will be held after the coaching process is complete, to identify the changes in the client's leadership behavior.

STEP 3: DEFINE THE CLIENT'S SHORT-, MEDIUM-, AND LONG-TERM OBJECTIVES

Once you have held the triad meeting to identify the key stakeholders' objectives, the coaching can focus on helping the client build his or her awareness and insight. Follow the steps below to define the client's short-, medium-, and long-term objectives:

- Have the client complete a series of psychometric inventories to identify his or her preferred decision-making style, type of creativity and learning style, preferred team role, and preferred leadership style. The objective of these inventories is to develop the client's self-awareness, which is a precursor to social awareness.

- Develop a picture of the client's personal vision (e.g., explore the client's personal values, the organization's work structure, and employees' behavior; craft an organizational vision).

- To enhance the client's relationship with the boss, identify the boss's needs, ambitions, and fears and how best to support him or her.

- Develop a SWOT analysis (i.e., **s**trengths, **w**eaknesses, **o**pportunities, and **t**hreats) of the organizational portfolio, services, or products that the client is responsible for and how the information ties into the company's overall goals.

- Analyze the team and what each direct report might need to be more productive and effective. The coach's intention is to develop the leader's agility in using an array of leadership styles. Have the client theoretically apply the psychometric inventories to his or her direct reports to identify how best to communicate and support each of them.

- Review the organization's desired competencies and management abilities. You may relate the client's development to the competencies.

TAKING OFF THE BLINDERS TO HAVE A HELICOPTER VIEW
Stakeholder Awareness

STEP 4: COACH FROM THE CURRENT SITUATION

In your work with clients, focus on coaching from the current situation. Work with the client to resolve interpersonal problems he or she is currently facing, and track his or her progress. Create insight by having the client analyze his or her direct reports according to what was learned with the psychometric inventories in order to enhance the client's communication.

Coworker Action Research Report: Interview Process

In preparation for conducting the Coworker Action Research Report interviews, complete the following steps:

- Ask the client to compile a list of respected interviewees he or she wants feedback from.
- Add two to four anonymous stakeholders (e.g., new employees, customers) to the list, with input from human resources or the client's boss if need be.
- Reassure the coaching client (verbally and in the coaching agreement) that no one else will see the report.
- Give the client the prototype letter to send to participants.

When conducting the interviews, follow the steps below:

- Schedule stakeholder interviews.
- Repeat at each interview that the information given is confidential and that no identifying material will be included in the report.
- Let respondents know they may add or delete information later if they choose.

- Continue to interview stakeholders until the information from the interviews becomes redundant.
- Identify the client's protectors and defenders.

As you write the Coworker Action Research Report summarizing how the client's leadership behavior is perceived by others, use the steps below as a guide:

- If more than one person conducted the interviews, combine the interviewers' notes about the client's leadership behaviors.
- Regroup similar observations by the different respondents into patterns or categories.
- Take out any identifying material (e.g., lingo, specific examples).
- Suggest specific action steps with the client that could be implemented to alter negative perceptions and leverage positive attributes.
- Identify coaching questions that could be addressed after the Coworker Action Research Report debriefing session.
- Develop an action plan from the Coworker Action Research Report.

STEP 5: CREATE A VISION OF THE CLIENT'S DESIRED FUTURE

Once the Coworker Action Research Report is complete, use it to guide the client in building a clear vision of the personal outcome he or she desires over the long term and how it aligns with the organization. Define what the client wants to learn from his or her situation. As you debrief the report with the client and proceed with coaching, keep the following steps in mind:

- Ask the client about his or her background. Identify any unmet needs by examining significant events in the client's early development. Formulate a hypothesis about the client's current and past aspirations and frustrations to better understand the system he or she lives in and what might have provoked him or her to start reacting defensively and abrasively.

- Identify whether a chronic pattern of abrasive behavior emerged from the Coworker Action Research Report.

- Debrief with the client the patterns and themes that emerged from the Coworker Action Research Report.

- Review with the client what his or her long-term goals are, then guide the client in analyzing which of his or her behavior patterns are conducive to reaching those goals and which might be impeding him or her from reaching them. Discuss what the client needs to change to reach his or her goals faster and more productively.

- If relevant, ask the client whether and how the negative perceptions in the Coworker Action Research Report are hindering him or her from reaching his or her desired goals.

- Have the client do a SWOT analysis of his or her career.

- Ask the client to decide what negative perceptions he or she wants to change and how best to leverage his or her strengths.

- Help the client identify quick and easy action steps he or she can implement immediately to address the negative perceptions.

- Work with the client to identify any consequences or threats that might ensue from not tackling an issue, before he or she decides not to address a negative perception that might hurt his or her career.

- Explore with the client different assumptions about why stakeholders have negative perceptions of him or her. Drill down to very specific behaviors or attitudes that project these negative perceptions.

- Explore with the client the deeper issues underlying his or her angry outbursts, to develop self-awareness and insight and address some of the client's unmet underlying needs.

- Help the client learn to manage negative perceptions and develop strategies to counter those perceptions.
- Review and identify how best to leverage the client's strengths in different business contexts.

DRAFTING A CLEAR JOURNEY TO THE DESIRED END
With More Self Awareness and Empathy, Integrating New Behavior

STEP 6: UNDERSTAND THE GAP BETWEEN THE CURRENT SITUATION AND THE DESIRED OUTCOME

Next, it's important to help the client understand the gap between his or her current situation and the desired outcome. Then, start to develop a plan for how that gap will be bridged. The Coworker Action Research Report is a valuable tool in this process.

- Debrief patterns and categories with the client. Help him or her develop a different assumptions about the cause of the feedback.
- Identify with the client what behaviors he or she will change to get a better reaction and perception from respondents and to reduce the gap between his or her goals and the current challenges.
- If a client is resistant to change, review the possible consequences of not addressing the behavior.
- Begin with the easiest behavior changes for immediate results.
- Once the first changes have been made, coach the client on the selected behavior changes that remain and are more challenging.

FROM A BRILIANT JERK TO A BRILLIANT LEADER WITH A POWERFUL VISION
Organizational Awarenesss

STEP 7: IDENTIFY THE CLIENT'S INSIGHTS AND KEY TAKEAWAYS

At the end of each coaching session, review with the client the insights he or she gained during the session, as well as the session's key lessons.

Applying Self-Awareness, Boss Awareness and Organizational Awareness to Craft a Compelling and Inspiring Vision that is Powerful

STEP 8: CREATE AN ACTION PLAN TO IMPLEMENT BEFORE THE NEXT SESSION

This work is primarily the client's responsibility, although the coach will help manage progress and accountability.

STEP 9: CONDUCT BRIEF STAKEHOLDER INTERVIEWS

Six to nine months after the coaching process is complete, hold mini-interviews with the same key stakeholders to identify how their perception of the client has changed. Debrief this feedback with the client.

STEP 10: HOLD ANOTHER TRIAD MEETING

Near the close of the coaching process, facilitate another triad meeting with the client, the boss and HR, and the coach to identify progress the client has made and determine next steps.

Chapter Notes

Introduction

1   Paul Babiak and Robert D. Hare, *Snakes in Suits: When Psychopaths Go to Work* (New York: HarperCollins, 2006).
Stanley Bing, *Crazy Bosses: Spotting Them, Serving Them, Surviving Them* (New York: Morrow, 1992).
Robert I. Sutton, *The No Asshole Rule: Building a Civilized Workplace and Surviving One That Isn't* (New York: Business Plus/Hachette, 2007).

2   Jean Lipman-Blumen, *The Allure of Toxic Leaders: Why We Follow Destructive Bosses and Corrupt Politicians—and How We Can Survive Them* (Oxford, UK: Oxford University Press, 2005).
Judith A. Richman et al., "Workplace Harassment, Active Coping, and Alcohol-Related Outcomes," *Journal of Substance Abuse* 13, no. 3 (2001): 347–366.

3   Laura Crawshaw, *Taming the Abrasive Manager: How to End Unnecessary Roughness in the Workplace* (San Francisco: Jossey-Bass, 2005).

4   Robert I. Sutton, *The No Asshole Rule.*

5   Solomon Markos Kompaso and M. Sandhya Sridevi, "Employee Engagement: The Key to Improving Performance," *International Journal of Business and Management* 5, no. 12 (2010): 89–96.

6   Marco Tavanti, "Managing Toxic Leaders: Dysfunctional Patterns in Organizational Leadership and How to Deal With Them," *Human Resource Management* 83, no 6 (2011): 127–136.

Chapter 3

1   Walter Bradford Cannon, *Bodily Changes in Pain, Hunger, Fear, and Rage* (New York: Appleton-Century-Crofts, 1929).
Henk van't Klooster, "Adrenaline: Fight or Flight Response" [video], November 22, 2012. Retrieved March 27, 2017, from https://www.youtube.com/watch?v=FBnBTkcr6No.

2   Laura Crawshaw, "The Science and Practice of Coaching Abrasive Executives." Workshop presented in Crans-Montana, Switzerland, November 30–December 3, 2009.

3   "Managing Stress" [video], BBC, July 14, 2010. Retrieved March 27, 2017, from https://www.youtube.com/watch?v=hnpQrMqDoqE.

4   Nathanael J. Fast and Serena Chen, "When the Boss Feels Inadequate: Power, Incompetence, and Aggression," *Psychological Science* 20 (2009): 1406–1413.

CHAPTER 4

1   Bonnie Low-Kramen, "Workplace Bullying: The #1 Workplace Problem That No One Talks About," Glassdoor, October 31, 2014. https://www.glassdoor.com/blog/workplace-bullying-1-workplace-problem-talks/.
Society for Human Resource Management, "Workplace Bullying Policy," May 23, 2014, https://www.shrm.org/resourcesandtools/tools-and-samples/policies/pages/cms_018350.aspx.

2   B. S. McEwen, "Central Effects of Stress Hormones in Health and Disease: Understanding the Protective and Damaging Effects of Stress and Stress Mediators," *European Journal of Pharmacology* 583 (2008): 174–185.

A. DeLongis, S. Folkman, and R. S. Lazarus, "The Impact of Daily Stress on Health and Mood: Psychological and Social Resources as Mediators," *Journal of Personality and Social Psychology* 54 (1988): 486–495.

3   Bruce S. McEwen, "Central Effects of Stress Hormones in Health and Disease."

4   A. M. Hansen et al., "Bullying at Work, Health Outcomes, and Physiological Stress Response," *Journal of Psychosomatic Research* 60, no. 1 (2006): 63–72.

5   A. Hogh, H. Hoel, and I. Carneiro, "Bullying and Employee Turnover Among Healthcare Workers: A Three-Wave Prospective Study," *Journal of Nursing Management* 19 (2011): 742–751.

6   Michael M. Lombardo and Morgan W. McCall, *Coping With an Intolerable Boss: Special Report* (Greensboro, NC: Center for Creative Leadership, 1984).
Michael M. Lombardo and Morgan W. McCall, "The Intolerable Boss," *Psychology Today* 9 (1984, January): 45–48.

7   Benjamin Snyder, "Half of Us Have Quit Our Job Because of a Bad Boss," *Fortune*, April 2, 2015, http://fortune.com/2015/04/02/quit-reasons/.

CHAPTER 5

1   Society for Human Resource Management, "Workplace Bullying Policy," May 23, 2014, https://www.shrm.org/resourcesandtools/tools-and-samples/policies/pages/cms_018350.aspx.

CHAPTER 7

1 Laura Crawshaw, *Taming the Abrasive Manager: How to End Unnecessary Roughness in the Workplace* (San Francisco: Jossey-Bass, 2007).

2 International Coach Federation, "Core Competencies," https://www.coachfederation.org/credential/landing.cfm?ItemNumber=2206.

CHAPTER 8

1 Laura Crawshaw, "Coaching Abrasive Leaders: Using Action Research to Reduce Suffering and Increase Productivity in Organizations," *International Journal of Coaching in Organization* 29, no. 8 (2010): 60–77.

CHAPTER 13

1 Ken Blanchard, "Situational Leadership II," http://www.kenblanchard.com/Products-Services/Leadership-Fundamentals/Situational-Leadership-II. Daniel Goleman, "Leadership That Gets Results."

About the Author

DR. KATRINA BURRUS, MCC[1], BCC[2], has a proven track record in coaching numerous international leaders, in top organizations like Nestlé, Novartis, United Bank of Switzerland, CERN, United Nations, and the International Labor Organization. Her coaching career has taken her to Europe, Asia, and the United States, and she is recognized for her distinctive capabilities with leaders and teams from a wide variety of cultural backgrounds.

As the founder of MKB Conseil & Coaching in Geneva, Switzerland, and Excellent Executive Coaching, LLC, in Las Vegas, Nevada, she has developed a powerful network of international clients, experts and scholar-practitioners.

Dr. Burrus has taught leadership and postgraduate courses at various universities, including a ground-breaking thought leadership workshop entitled, *Global Nomadic Leadership: Succeeding in a World Without Borders.* She teaches executive coaching and has served on the International Coach Federation (ICF) Credentialing Committee.

Dr. Burrus was the first ICF master certified coach in Switzerland. She is a founder and Board Member of ICF Switzerland and served on the editorial board of the *International Journal of Coaching in Organizations.* She was also a start-up coach for the Swiss government.

Dr. Burrus' most popular leadership programs and signature speeches include:

---

1   ICF stands for International Coach Federation.
2   BCC stands for Board Certified Coach.

- Managing Brilliant Jerks: How Organizations and Coaches Can Transform a Difficult Leader into a Powerful Visionary
- How to Fast Track to the C-Suite and Beyond
- How to Thrive in a Global Corporate Culture

Made in the USA
Las Vegas, NV
09 August 2021

27852881R00144